Tree Time Living On Nature's Clock

Where the Fields Meet the Years

Geoffrey Yoder

Editors

Rachel Arterberry at Making A Way Writing Services

https://www.makingawaywriting.com

Sandra Connelly: Retired NASA Senior Executive

eBook ISBN: 979-8-9987404-7-3

Paperback : 979-8-9987404-8-0

Hardcover: 979-8-9987404-9-7

Cover Photo: Credit: Lauretta Yoder

Contents

Dedication

Many Influences

A Mosaic of Influence and Gratitude

Life is an intricate masterpiece, woven together by countless threads, each representing a person, a memory, or a lesson that shapes who we become. At the heart of this tapestry lies dedication: the quiet force that binds us to our values, our loved ones, and the communities that nurture us. As I reflect on my journey, I am reminded that no individual walks this path alone. The people and traditions that have touched my life have not only guided me but also taught me the enduring power of love, resilience, and shared purpose. It is with profound gratitude that I offer this book to all who seek inspiration in the face of life's challenges, a tribute to the hands that lifted me, the voices that sustained me, and the hearts that continue to light my way.

The Legacy of my Grandfather

Among the early threads not in this story but still a figure of stability in my life is my late grandfather, a man whose hands spoke a language of patience and precision. I worked side by side with him during one of my first jobs at a meat packing plant. I would spend weekends with my grandfather in his wood shop, where the scent of sawdust mingled with the warmth of afternoon sunlight, I learned the compassion of grace. Together, we built flower stands, carved simple yet elegant pieces, and, in those moments, he taught me that dedication is not merely about the finished product but the care poured into every stroke of the chisel. But more than that, his shop became a sanctuary for conversations about life, about perseverance in the face of hardship, the importance of humility, and the beauty of small, deliberate acts of kindness. These lessons, passed down through calloused hands and gentle wisdom, instilled in me a reverence for craftsmanship and a deep respect for the time-honored value of hard work. My grandfather's influence remains a cornerstone of my identity, a reminder that dedication is a legacy built one moment at a time.

Sibling Bonds and the Strength of Support

As I grew, the role of my sister became another vital thread in the fabric of my life. She was there, steadfast and unwavering, during my later years, offering a shoulder to lean on when the weight of life's trials felt too heavy to bear alone. Her presence taught me that true dedication is not always grand or loud; often, it is the quiet, steady support of a sibling who knows when to listen and when to act. Through her compassion, I discovered the strength found in vulnerability, the courage required to accept help, and the profound comfort of knowing someone will remain by your side through every season of life. Her love, both fierce and subtle, shaped my understanding of what it means to care deeply for another and to be cared for in return.

The Steadfast Anchor of Partnership

No reflection on dedication would be complete without honoring my wife, Lauretta, whose unwavering presence has been the steady anchor of my journey. Through the unpredictable tides of life, moments of triumph and periods of struggle, she has stood beside me with quiet strength, her hand always ready, her heart always open. Her dedication is not found in grand gestures but in the everyday choices: the conversations when doubts kept us awake, the encouragement when I faltered, the laughter that restored joy on weary days. To share a life is to share its burdens and its wonders, and I have been immeasurably lucky to navigate this path with someone who champions me without reservation. Her love, a living testament to the power of commitment, has been the cornerstone of my resilience.

Family: A Legacy of Love and Joy

The circle of life expanded with the arrival of my son, Eugene, and his beloved wife, Clara. In them, I see the continuation of values I once admired in others: compassion, integrity, and an abiding love for family. Their dedication to each other and to us, their parents, has deepened my faith in the enduring nature of love that transcends generations. Eugene and Clara have embraced their roles with grace, balancing the demands of raising a family while nurturing the bonds that tie us together. A true joy in this extended family is our grandson, Bryton, a whirlwind of energy, creativity, and curiosity. With a passion for hockey and a heart full of kindness, he embodies the best of both generations, a reminder that life's challenges are met not with fear but with enthusiasm and grit. In Bryton's eyes, I see the future, bright, untamed, and full of promise, and I am reminded daily of the joy found in witnessing the growth of those we hold dear.

The Heartbeat of Community

Beyond my immediate family, the community that raised me remains an indelible part of my story. In the small towns and neighborhoods where I grew up, life was rich with traditions that celebrated connection and simplicity: the soulful harmonies of four-part singing ringing through church halls, the meticulous craftsmanship of woodwork passed from one generation to the next, and the comforting aroma of freshly baked bread from the local bakery. These shared rituals taught me that dedication is not only a personal virtue but a communal one, a collective effort to preserve the beauty of heritage, to uplift one another, and to find meaning in everyday moments. The teachers, neighbors, and friends who shaped my early years instilled in me a love for the little things: a handshake that conveys respect, a shared meal that speaks of care, a song that unites voices in harmony. Their influence reminds me that no one achieves their full potential in isolation; we rise together, strengthened by the bonds of those around us.

A Dedication to the Journey Ahead

This book is a testament to the belief that life, in all its complexity, is a journey best faced with courage, gratitude, and an open heart. It is dedicated to those who have walked beside me and to all who will one day read these words. May they find solace in knowing they are not alone, may they draw strength from the hands that will inevitably lift them, and may they carry forward the lessons of dedication, love, and perseverance. For every challenge that lies ahead, know this: there are those who believe in you, who have walked similar paths, and who will continue to light the way. As I have been shaped by the love and example of my family and community, so too can you be inspired to forge your own path, knowing that even in the darkest moments, the light of human connection will endure.

To my wife Lauretta, Eugene, Clara, Bryton, my sister, my grandfather, and the countless others who have touched my life, thank you. Your dedication has left an indelible mark.

Praise for the Book

Pre-Release Comments

Summary of Comments from Pre-Release Reviewers

In the quiet cadence of his memoir, Geoff unspools his boyhood summers spent chasing dragonflies over sun-warmed fields, the crisp autumn mornings when leaves fell like whispered promises, the stark, breath-free winters that turned the world to glass, and the hopeful bloom of spring that coaxed buds from the frozen Earth. Now, as an adult, he watches those same seasonal rhythms echo through his own life-each youthful exuberance (a bright summer), the inevitable losses that strip him to his core (a melancholy fall), the solitary hours of doubt (a winter of the soul), and the moments of renewal (new love, fresh purpose, reclaimed dreams)—a perennial spring that reminds him that, just as nature cycles without fail, so too does the human heart, forever turning, ever resilient, finding meaning in the relentless procession of change.

Geoff's book is a truly inspiring read, filled with stories that touch the heart. Raised on a small farm, Geoff learned so much from the land's changing seasons. Spring showed him how to plant seeds of hope in rich, fertile soil. Summer taught him the importance of being patient, working hard through both good times and tough droughts. Autumn brought the joy of seeing his hard work pay off. And winter reminded him that sometimes, all you need is to sit back and be still. Each of these cycles, with its challenges and rewards, was like a reflection of his own life, helping him build resilience and a deep respect for the earth's quiet, powerful strength.

Chapter One

Prologue

Seasons of Our Life

To See the Forest, You Must First Understand the Trees

As I stepped out of the house, I headed toward a muddy path that was used by tractors to move from one field to another. My feet were slipping in the wheel tracks, and I didn't mind if mud covered my shoes; I was on a mission. Cows in the field beside the path came running to the fence to see what I was up to. Was I bringing them food? Several cows mooed in anticipation of something new, but they lost interest when they realized I was just walking. When I got to the edge of the hay field, I stopped to look back at the house to see if anyone was watching me. I was convinced I was alone, so I continued my journey through the cornfield. I briefly rested at a lonely birch tree halfway down the cornfield, wondering why this tree was still standing. Was it a boundary marker? Was it left there for shade? I peeled a small section of flat, thin bark, thinking this might have been used as paper for settlers. I moved on to the next field, getting closer to my destination. Now, less than 400 yards away, I stopped at a small spring of water shaded by several trees, wondering if the water ever stopped flowing. It seemed strange that the spring was on the edge of an open field. Did the farmers decide the field boundaries around the spring, or did the spring appear after the field was in place? Within sight, I continued walking until I reached the woods on the edge of our property. As I stepped in among the trees, the air buzzed with life; sunlight filtered through a canopy of leaves, painting the ground in dappled gold. From afar, the woods felt like a single, breathing entity, a vast, green heart pulsing with mystery.

True understanding didn't come from just admiring the horizon. It started with a single step into the undergrowth, where the secrets of the whole lay waiting in the details. To really understand the woods, I needed to first kneel beside a tree, trace the lines of its bark, listen to its whispered stories, and recognize its unique role in the symphony of life.

Each tree is like its own little world. Think about an oak tree at the edge of the forest, its trunk reaching up high, defying gravity and time. Then there's a young sapling, so fragile and new, showing real bravery, a tiny shoot reaching for the light, even when shadows try to hold it back. They're not just parts of the forest; they're its poets, architects, and protectors. When I look at just one tree, I see not only how special it is but also how it talks to the world, a conversation that keeps the whole ecosystem going. The strange branch shapes, knots in odd places, dead branches next to healthy ones, ants walking around like they're using the tree as a home. Why does a young sapling grow next to an older tree?

Think about this in terms of our own lives. When we work together to make our dreams come true, we shine because of all the effort we put in. Just as an orchestra makes a beautiful sound not only at the big finish, but with each musician playing their part, a city feels alive not because of its buildings, but the baker making dough at dawn, the teacher sparking curiosity, and the engineer fixing the roads. If we forget the little things, the special details, and what seems unimportant, we might miss the harmony that makes everything amazing.

No forest is strong with just one kind of tree; it's the mix of oaks, maples, pines, and ferns that keeps it balanced. Our differences, our special skills, ways of seeing things, and challenges are the roots that make our society strong. To help us grow as people, we need to appreciate each person's unique talent; it's in their special light that we can all shine together.

When things get complicated, take a deep breath and really look at them. Find the one thing that makes you special, the unique connection you have, and the skill that's all yours. Give it your full attention, care, and respect. When you focus on understanding your own "tree", your role, your craft, your purpose, you become a vital part of something bigger. Your roots will connect with others, sharing strength and stories. Together, you'll create a thriving ecosystem where life grows, dreams take root, and the future is full of endless possibilities. This is just a peek into my own journey of finding my "tree" in the big forest of life.

Looking back at the trees

As I entered retirement and into a comforting routine of daily tasks and occasional bursts of unexpected joy, the days are no longer consumed by the relentless demands of deadlines and late emails; instead, they unfold like familiar notes in a song, one after another. Occasionally, a particular scent, a distinct sound, or a gentle beam of light transports me back to a time when the world felt like a living storybook, with each leaf a page and each sunrise a new chapter. These moments serve as a poignant reminder that growing older is not about closing doors, but rather about opening windows so that we can still behold the enchantment of our younger days.

Where I grew up

I grew up on a small farm on the edge of a sprawling woods, a patchwork of ancient pines, trembling birches, and stubborn oaks that seemed to hold the sky in their gnarled branches. The woods were not a backdrop; it was a character, sometimes mischievous, sometimes solemn, always present. In the spring, the pines exhaled a sharp, resinous perfume that clung to my shirt as I chased a wayward mouse through the dew-slick grass. In the summer, the birches whispered in a language I could not yet name, their white bark flashing like moonlit sails against the green canopy. In the autumn, the oaks shed their amber crowns in a slow, reverent cascade, and I would sit beside their exposed roots, a blanket of leaves crackling beneath me, feeling the earth pulse with the rhythm of the seasons. Winter turned the forest into a cathedral of silence, the snow muffling every footfall until even the wind seemed to hold its breath.

The woods have given me more wisdom than any book ever could. They showed me patience; it takes years for a little acorn to grow into a big oak. They also taught me to be humble, like the tall pines that bend down under a storm just as gently as a child's hand. They sparked my curiosity; every little noise in the bushes hinted at a hidden creature, maybe a shy fox, a shy hedgehog, or the twinkling glow of fireflies that turned the night into a starry wonderland. Most of all, they taught me to respect nature. The forest was like a living library, each tree a story, each moss-covered stone a footnote, each bird call a reminder to see the world with my heart.

Now as I enter the later seasons of my life, I'm no longer out in the fields and trees, but in a small office in our countryside home, a four-hour drive from where I grew up. My desk is now just a dresser top instead of my usual office desk, where I would write review papers or hold video calls. It's a gentle reminder that a dresser can be turned into a place of imagination without losing its charm. As I sit here, the stories I had as a child still ring true, echoing through the fan's hum, the rustle of papers, and the soft patter of rain on the glass.

It's fascinating how a simple, unexpected moment can whisk you away to another time. My wife opened a container of scented incense, and as the fragrance filled the room, I was instantly back in the woods, helping my father fix a barbed wire fence to keep the cattle from wandering off our farm. I remembered the sting of accidentally grabbing the barbed part of the wire and seeing blood trickle from my hand. My father laughed as we continued repairing the fence. I bet he felt the same pain of grabbing the barbed wire when he was younger. In that moment, I felt the same steady breath of the forest that steadied my father's hands, and I realized that the calm I now have in retirement is the same calm I once drew from the ancient trees.

Another afternoon, the soft trill of a bird perched on the bird feeders on the edge of our patio reminded me of the first time I heard a whole chorus of birds, sitting in line on the power lines near the farmhouse, each note a promise that the day would be filled with possibilities. The sound lifted me out of watching a documentary and into the memory of a sunrise in our farmhouse yard where I stood barefoot on the damp earth, feeling the pulse of life beneath my soles.

These sensory bridges are more than just a trip down memory lane; they're the threads that connect the pieces of who we are. They remind me that the responsibilities I carried throughout my career, leading organizations, mentoring the next generation of students, sharing my NASA experiences for encouragement, are not separate tasks but extensions of the lessons the forest once shared. The patience I learned from watching a sapling push through tough soil guided me when I felt like I was hitting a wall. The humility I felt under the weight of a storm-bent pine helps me listen when an elder shares a story that, at first glance, seems unrelated to current policies. The curiosity that once sent me chasing fireflies has since led me to explore new technologies and adventures.

As we get older, one of the most amazing things we realize is that routine doesn't have to be boring; it can be a blank canvas where surprises can really shine. In my little office, which is now part of our guest bedroom, I have a small bookshelf that my great-grandfather helped my father build from wood cut from the trees on our farm. It reminds me of sitting by that bookshelf as a kid, chatting on a CB radio with my friends every night. You can still see the two mounting holes on the front where I placed the CB microphone. I've refinished the bookshelf, bringing it back to its original look. My father, living in an assisted living home, wanted to change the color. The assisted living community didn't allow residents to paint inside their rooms, so, always finding ways to work around rules, my father decided to use different kinds of jelly for the paint. Yep, you heard that right; grape jelly for the blue, raspberry jelly for the red, and so on. He thought it was a masterpiece. But, well, to me it was a disaster. Luckily, no critters were drawn to the jelly-covered bookshelf.

Bookshelf that my father and grand-father built

On clear nights, I stand by the window and watch the sun dip below the horizon, imagining it hiding behind the mountain trees and hills of my childhood. The leaves turning the ordinary into a cathedral of amber and feeling the same sense of wonder that once made me believe the world was a storybook, each day a new page to turn.

Sometimes, the everyday becomes something truly magical, showing me that age doesn't take away our sense of wonder; it makes it even stronger.

A few weeks ago, I was driving through the winding roads of Connecticut at night when I saw a big deer right in front of me. I had to stop to avoid hitting it, and its antlers sparkled in my car headlights. In that moment, I felt the forest come alive: playful, as if the deer winked at us; serious, as it slowly walked into the woods, reminding me of the delicate balance we try to protect; and present, it had chosen that exact moment to cross our paths.

Looking back on these moments, I've realized that inspiration really comes from the quiet flow between what's past and what's happening now. The farm's red barn, the forest's rustling leaves, the hum of the office printer, each is a note in a bigger song that's been playing since I first learned to tie my shoes on the porch of our farmhouse. When I let myself listen to that music, feel every sound, I find a source of purpose that keeps me steady, even as I get older.

So, when the calendar turns to another number in the sixties or even later, I don't feel sad about losing my youth; I celebrate all the moments that have made me who I am, a mosaic of stories, each piece shining with its own color. I'm also reminded that the world still has chapters waiting to be written. The forest is still there, patient and ready, waiting for new people to walk on its mossy floor. The farm, though damaged by two tornadoes, still gives, offering new chances to grow food sustainably. And my little office, with its bookshelf built by my father and grandfather, is still a door that lets others step back into that living storybook.

In the end, the rhythm of routine isn't a cage but a metronome, keeping time for the heartbeats of all the moments that have shaped us. The occasional surprise, a scent, a sound, a flicker of light, acts as the unexpected refrain that reminds us to listen, to remember, and to keep turning the pages with reverence and joy. And as I sit here, pen in hand (not really, it is actually a computer keyboard), I feel a profound gratitude: for the forest that taught me to be present, for the farm that taught me to be resilient, and for the years that have allowed me to carry those lessons forward, inspiring not just myself but the generations that will follow down the same winding, leaf-strewn path.

Wandering Among the Trees

One of my first adventures started with a simple invitation: "Come walk in the woods."

I remember the feeling of soft moss beneath my shoes as it gently gave way to my steps, the way the air smelled of pine resin and damp earth, and how the canopy filtered sunlight into a kaleidoscope of gold and green. The woods were a symphony:

Birdsong: Warblers stitched melodies in the branches, their trills rivaling any concert hall. I learned the names of the birds not from textbooks but by matching their calls to the silhouettes that skimmed past me.

Deer at Play: In the clearing near the brook, I once watched a fawn wobble on its unsteady legs, while its mother lingered just beyond the trees, eyes alert yet calm.

Squirrels on the Run: Those quick, acrobatic critters turned every fallen nut into a game of hide-and-seek. I'd follow their zig-zagging routes, giggling when they'd dart up a trunk, as if daring me to keep up.

Even the brook itself was a mentor. Its water babbled over smooth stones, creating a rhythmic lullaby that seemed to say, "Take it slow, but keep moving."

I'd sit on a damp log, feet dangling, and toss pebbles, watching the ripples spread, an early lesson in cause and effect.

Midnight Musings Under a Blanket of Stars

When the sun slipped behind the horizon, the forest transformed. The night sky unfurled in a way that made the world feel both infinite and intimate. I would lie on a soft patch of grass, my back pressed against the cool earth, and stare up at the moon—sometimes a thin crescent, sometimes a luminous full disc.

The stars were not just points of light; they were stories. I learned to trace constellations with my finger, linking the pattern of Orion's belt to the hunter chasing across the heavens. The Milky Way, a milky river of galaxies, seemed to spill across the night, reminding me that the world was far larger than my little backyard.

Rain

There's something magical about a rainstorm in the countryside. The clouds roll in like a gray tide, and the first drops tap the tin roof of our farmhouse, making a crisp, high-pitched "tink-tink" that echoes through every room.

We'd press our faces against the window, watching the world turn glossy. The scent of wet soil rose, earthy and sweet, and the rhythm of the rain became a drumbeat for our imaginations. I'd imagine each drop as a tiny messenger, sliding down the roof to whisper secrets to the earth below.

Now, when I hear rain on a rural home's asphalt roof, my mind automatically drifts back to those tin-roof concerts.

I realize that the simple joy of listening, something I often took for granted, has become a rare, treasured ritual.

Snowflakes

In winter, I chased two snowflakes that looked so similar. I'd sit on the porch with a magnifying glass, collecting snowflakes on my mittens and lifting them to the light, intent on seeing every detail.

When I looked closer, I realized that each one was a unique and amazing piece of nature, so delicate, fleeting, and impossible to make again. This made me understand something important: the world is full of individuality, even in things that seem the same. Plus, it sparked a lifelong love for the patterns we see every day, like the veins in a leaf, the lines in a city, or even the way the sky looks.

Pond Hockey

When a frozen pond pops up, it turns into a huge ice rink! We put on our old skates, pushed a puck across the ice, and chased it with all the wild energy we had as kids. The cold bit at our faces, and our fingers and toes were numb, but the thrill and the sound of skates cutting through the ice made us feel like we could do anything.

What Those Memories Mean Today

Right now, sitting in my living room, I realize that the forest, the rain, the stars, the ice, and the snow are not just memories. They're the building blocks of how I see the world.

Being close to nature is super important to me, especially when we're always glued to screens and moving so fast. I often feel a strong pull toward nature, wanting to break away from the every-day and reconnect with the world's natural beauty. Whether it's a cruise in Alaska to see the amazing glaciers, diving into Alaskan culture, exploring the British Isles for a different cultural vibe, or a cruise in the Caribbean to enjoy the clear blue waters, each trip helps me understand how my simple life in the woods fits into the bigger picture of Earth.

Chapter Two

A Night of Wonder, Stillness, and Infinite Possibility

Under the Midnight Sky

There are those rare, precious moments when time seems to stand still, the world hushes, and the universe speaks in light, sound, and silence. When I was a teenager, under a sky so vast and open, untouched by city lights, I experienced one of those moments. Lying on cool, dew-kissed grass, wrapped in a soft blanket, I surrendered to the night, and the cosmos revealed its quiet beauty.

The sky was truly something else; crystal clear, deep indigo, alive with stars that felt like I was floating in the center of a galaxy. No light pollution to dull its beauty. No artificial glow to drown out the faint shimmer of distant suns. Just pure, unfiltered darkness, rich with mystery and wonder. The moon, full and luminous, rose slowly, like a pearl emerging from velvet. Its light was gentle, casting long, soft shadows across the pasture and illuminating the edges of the horizon.

Crickets sang their evening symphony, a rhythmic hum that pulsed through the still air. An owl called from beyond the barn, hoo-hoo, its haunting echo blending seamlessly with the night. And then, a deep, peaceful moo from across the field, as if the cows were whispering secrets to the stars. Nature wasn't separate; it was part of the moment, part of the harmony.

I lay there like a child with a storybook, breath even, heart calm, eyes tracing the constellations. There was the Little Dipper, small but proud, its handle curving toward Polaris, the North Star, steady, eternal, a celestial anchor. And nearby, the Big Dipper poured its imaginary contents across the sky, a cosmic ladle serving up wonder.

I searched for Orion, the great hunter, and found him rising in the east, his belt of three stars perfectly aligned, his sword faintly glowing. There, just above him, was a tiny, steady red speck: Mars, distant and mysterious, a world where rovers now roam and humans one day may walk.

And then, just as I was lost in deep thought, a streak of light appeared. A shooting star! Then another, and another. It was like a quiet meteor shower, unannounced and unplanned, painting quicksilver lines across the darkness. Each one seemed to whisper from the cosmos:

Photo credit: Greg Rakozy on Upsplash

Look up. You are not alone. You are part of something vast.

In that moment, I felt both incredibly small and deeply connected. I thought of Neil Armstrong and Buzz Aldrin, who stood where no human had ever stood before, gazing back at Earth as a tiny, pale blue dot. I imagined their awe, how the silence of the Moon must have spoken louder than any sound. I thought of the countless nights before me where humans had looked up and dreamed: of gods in constellations, of chariots drawn by stars, of messages written in light. I wondered whether my ancestors from Germany saw the same thing I was seeing. Did my great-grandfather pause to experience this marvel of the universe? And here I was, under the very same sky, dreaming still.

I started to connect the stars in my own way. Not the official constellations, but my own. A crooked line became the wings of an eagle. A scatter of faint lights shaped a galloping horse. I saw a cow, fitting, given the soft moos from the pasture, and imagined it grazing across the firmament. The night sky became my canvas, and my imagination, free from logic, painted stories only the soul could understand.

The owl called again. The crickets continued their song. The world remained alive, even under the spell of midnight. And as the moon climbed higher, I felt a deep sense of belonging, not to the land beneath me, but to something greater. I was small, yes, but so beautifully so. A single breath in the lungs of eternity.

As the silence settled back in, another meteor shower burst forth, more vivid, more frequent. Light streaks painted the sky like cosmic brushstrokes. Some disappeared quickly, while others glowed with golden trails that shimmered before vanishing. It felt like the universe, pleased with my quiet reverence, was offering a final gift: beauty unasked for, unearned, and freely given.

And slowly, so slowly, I almost didn't notice, I saw the first signs of dawn. Not with a bang, but with a softness that honored the night. Pale gold beams crept across a thin layer of fog that had gathered in the valley, turning the mist into glowing ribbons. The stars, once so bold, began to retreat, one by one, like shy guests leaving a long evening party. What had I just experienced? I wanted to revisit that feeling over and over again.

Birds stirred in the large pine trees surrounding the farmhouse. A dog barked in the distance, once, twice, awakening the quiet. Spiderwebs with their unique designs, draped between fence posts and grass tips, glistened with morning dew, each tiny drop catching the first light like a jewel. The air smelled of earth and pine and the coming rain.

As the sun continued to brighten the day, I noticed movement. Farmers began their day; tractors rumbled, lawn mowers hummed, and the clothes my mother had just washed now danced gently on a clothesline, fluttering like signals to the sky. Life, simple and grounded, resumed. But I carried the night with me.

My dog followed, nudging my hand now and then for a pet, his tail wagging, his eyes full of morning mischief. I paused, watching cloud formations shift overhead, some soft and cotton-like, others gathering into towering thunderheads. They, too, were telling stories: dragons, ships, mountains. My imagination, still awake from its celestial journey, saw them all.

Then the rain came, not in drops, but in music. Each raindrop unique, some fat and bold, others fine and hesitant, dancing on our house and shed tin roofs with a rhythm both chaotic and beautiful.

And I smiled.

As I looked back at the midnight sky adventure, I didn't just see stars; I remembered who I am. I felt connected to something ancient, like a witness to wonder and a dreamer under a sky so big.

In that moment of remembering, I found inspiration, a quiet, lasting kind that whispers:

Even if you feel small, remember you're noticed. Even if you're just a moment, you're part of something bigger. You can dream with the universe.

Lying on the cool, dew-kissed grass under a midnight sky is one of those rare moments when the universe leans in and whispers its oldest secrets. There's no grand ceremony, no fanfare, just you, the earth beneath your back, and an endless canopy of stars stretching into infinity. In that stillness, your breath slows, your thoughts quiet, and something deep within you awakens: a profound sense of awe, a humbling realization that you're just a single thread in the vast tapestry of existence.

This same reverence flooded me as a child wandering through a quiet woods. Sunlight pierced the canopy in golden shafts, illuminating moss-covered trunks that rose like pillars of a cathedral built by time itself. The oaks stood tall and wise, their gnarled branches stretching skyward as if in prayer. I reached out and touched one—rough bark beneath my fingers—and imagined the centuries it had witnessed: storms weathered, seasons turned, generations of creatures born and gone. Did my great-grandfather lean against this tree? Why was this tree still standing when other trees were cut down?

These trees had stood long before my grandparents' grandparents were born. They may have watched civilizations rise and fall, yet they remained—calm, rooted, enduring. I remember stopping in my tracks, overwhelmed not by fear, but by a deep, quiet respect. I was just a child, fleeting and small, beneath giants that time could not humble.

Both the starlit sky and the ancient forest remind us that greatness isn't just about how big something is, but how much it means to us. The universe doesn't make us feel small by showing us how small we are; it makes us feel free. Feeling small under the stars or the trees doesn't mean we're not important; it means we're part of something so huge and beautiful that it makes us wonder what's beyond what we can see.

In the quiet, I could hear my heartbeat echoing with the universe, and I felt a deep connection to something much bigger than myself, a feeling that still helps me when the modern world gets too loud.

And maybe that's the best thing about feeling awe: it makes us look beyond ourselves. It reminds us that we're part of something—this Earth, this moment, this ever-changing mystery. Whether we're watching stars that are older than any empire or standing under trees that have been around for ages, we're invited to listen, to breathe deeply, and to carry that quiet respect with us every day.

So, let's all take a blanket, lie down, and look up one night.

Let the crickets sing. Let the owls call. Let the stars tell their stories.

And in that vastness, we might just find ourselves, not lost, but found.

Chapter Three

A Journey Through the Heart of the Woods

Keep Your Mind Open

Wandering through the woods, like gazing at the starlit sky, evokes a profound dialogue between the soul and the universe. Time softens, blurring the boundaries between self and nature.

There's a special place where time feels like it's taking a break, and the noise of everyday life fades into a peaceful calm. This peaceful spot is filled with the soft rustle of leaves, the sweet songs of birds, and the gentle sound of a brook flowing over mossy rocks. It's a place that keeps calling me back, not just on a map, but deep inside me. The wooded area at the edge of our property, with its old fence and a big, old oak tree watching over it, is more than just trees. It's like a teacher, a safe place, and a mirror that shows us the way life moves.

I stepped into the woods, and the forest welcomed me. I started my walk beneath the wide, twisted branches of that huge, ancient oak. Its roots, spreading out like the hands of a wise old friend, seemed to hold the forest together, marking the line between the world we know and the wild. I touched its bark, rough, warm, alive, and took a deep breath. *Keep your mind open*, I told myself. That simple thought became my guide for the journey ahead.

Just past the oak, a narrow ravine cut through the earth, winding down into the depths of the woods. It was lined with the same rusted fence that kept the neighbor's cows in their pasture, their distant mooing a soft, grounding hum. I stopped, watching the sunlight dance through the leaves above. The fence stood as a boundary, not just of property, but of how we see things. On one side: order, predictability. On the other: mystery, surprise, wildness.

The path ahead was an old logging road, wide enough for a truck, now softened and overgrown by time. Moss covered the cracks between stones; ferns reached up from the edges like green hands inviting me to come closer. As I walked, I realized how hard it is really to "see the forest through the trees." So often, life throws us so much detail, endless tasks, emotions, and distractions that it hides the bigger picture. But here, the forest whispered: Slow down. Breathe. Let the details lead you to the whole.

As I walked along the path, I came upon a peaceful stream. The water looked so still, it barely disturbed the smooth pebbles, but it was alive with the gentle sound of flowing water. I found a flat rock to rest my knee on, cupped my hands, and took a refreshing sip. The water was cool and pure, making me think of the Earth, sky, and ancient stone. It quenched my thirst and cleared my mind. I looked up and saw sunlight filtering through the leaves, golden and fleeting, like little gifts from the branches.

Birdsong filled the air. Chickadees chirped from the maples, a woodpecker drummed a rhythm on a dead pine, and crows cawed from the treetops, their voices sharp and clear. It felt like they were saying, "This is our place." I smiled, feeling like I was visiting, humbled, and amazed. A squirrel zipped across my path and then jumped behind me, quick flashes of brown and white against the green. For a moment, we were both moving with the same energy.

Then, everything went quiet. Not silent, but a deep quiet that felt like time had stopped. I leaned against a birch tree, its bark peeling like old letters, and looked around at the trees: the strong oak, the graceful maple, the tall ash, and the delicate birch. Each one was unique and important. I now look back and think about how rare it is to truly notice things in life. We rush around, always looking at screens or thinking about the future, and rarely see the beautiful details right in front of us.

But the forest always wants us to be present.

Then, the sting; it was real!

I accidentally stepped on a bee's nest. Suddenly, the world went into a wild hum. I ran, swatting my arms, my heart racing, to a deep-water hole where I dove in, hoping the water would shield me. The bees, undeterred by my swatting, seemed to say, "You messed with us, now leave." But not before a dozen stings, no, more, burned into my skin. I later counted over a hundred. I laughed through the pain. Even in the toughest moments, there was a lesson: nature doesn't judge. It just is. I had upset its balance, and it responded. Not out of anger, but out of necessity.

And yet, even then, as I sat cooling my stung body in the water, I felt a sense of wonder. The forest wasn't punishing me; it was teaching me. How beautifully the elements work together: water, air, insects, trees, and wind. Each plays a part. The bees protect their home. The water offers healing. The wind carries the scent of pine and the rustle of leaves like a lullaby.

I continued walking through the woods and found a beech tree with vines that invited me to swing, laughing like a child, kicking up the air. Nearby, a narrow path led along a ledge, a path that I had walked many times with my father, looking over a hidden grove where a pine tree, gnarly and full of fruit, grew beside a gentle brook. I carefully walked across the mossy stones, balancing like a ballet dancer to avoid slipping. Underneath, tiny tadpoles darted around like little drops of ink. Life, in its smallest forms, was pulsing beneath the calm. I continued my adventure from the brook to a quiet part of the woods.

Eventually, I found a pine grove. The ground was covered with needles, soft as a carpet, releasing a sharp, sweet fragrance with every step. I stood there, breathed deeply, feeling the quiet strength of the pines. Further on, I crawled through a briar patch, thorns catching at my sleeves, cutting into my hands, to reach a cluster of wild blackberries. I ate them straight from the vine; juicy, tart, staining my fingers purple. A small reward for my persistence.

Time slipped by unnoticed. The light shifted from golden to amber, signaling it was time to head home. I paused at the top of a steep field and rolled a large stone down the hill just for the sheer joy of watching it tumble, listening to its echo before beginning my journey. I continued to a familiar stream to quench my thirst. I rested at a rugged, three-sided shelter, a relic from someone long ago, perhaps built for the same reason I was there: refuge. The shelter's weathered boards, with gaps between each, became a haven for many visits to the woods. The exhaustion of what felt like miles of walking home settled into my bones, but it was a good tired, earned, and honest.

I crossed open fields of hay and corn, the tall stalks whispering in the evening breeze. They seemed to say, "This is our place, but you are welcome to our home." Crickets began their song, and the sky blazed with the last fire of sunset.

But as I turned back, I saw it, the forest. Not just trees, paths, or streams, but a living, breathing whole. I had walked through the details for what felt like miles, consumed by each moment, each sensation. Only now, as I stepped away, could I truly see the forest.

And as I walked, I reflected.

The forest had given me more than beauty. It had given me perspective. Amid life's thickets, the stress, the noise, the endless to-do lists, it's easy to lose sight of the whole. We focus on the branch in front of us and forget the tree. We fixate on the sting and miss the healing water. But when we keep our minds open, when we walk slowly and listen deeply, we begin to see the patterns, the connections, the quiet wisdom woven through every leaf, every stone, every breath.

I didn't just walk through the woods. I walked into them and out the other side, changed.

And the greatest gift? Not the berries, or the view, or even the sunrise through the trees.

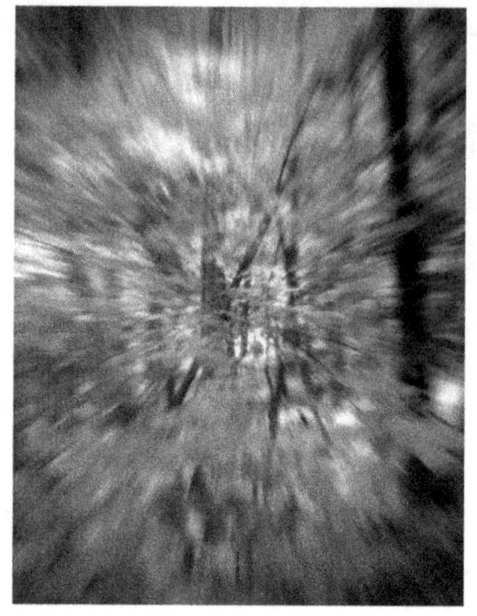

It was the reminder:

Sometimes, to see the forest, you first must lose yourself in the trees.

As you step away, with your mind open and heart full, you see it all, not just as a place, but as a part of you.

I walked through the woods many times as a child, each step a whisper of memory etched into the Earth and my soul. Those quiet paths, framed by ancient trees and dappled sunlight, taught me more about life than any classroom ever could. For in their stillness, the woods revealed the poetry of time, written in the language of the seasons.

So, when life feels uncertain or heavy, I close my eyes and walk those woods again. I remember: every winter ends. Every spring returns. And every step forward, no matter the season, is sacred.

Chapter Four

The Symphony of Seasons

"To everything there is a season, and a time for every purpose under the heavens." – Ecclesiastes 3:1 (KJV)

As I reminisced about my journeys through the woods as a child, I couldn't shake the feeling that time itself was heavy on my shoulders. The trees stood like wise old guardians, their skeletal branches reaching toward a pale winter sky. In that moment, a memory surfaced, a blend of past walks through the same woods, each season adding its own unique touch. Winter's quiet, spring's gentle whisper, summer's joyful laughter, and autumn's final graceful dance. Each season, distinct yet connected, had painted its own story on my heart. Together, they create a masterpiece that reminds me of life's fleeting beauty and enduring grace. Let me take you on this journey through time and the changing of the earth.

If the forest were a teacher, the seasons would be its lessons.

Spring arrived with a burst of green, and the world seemed to exhale. New buds transformed into blossoms, and the air buzzed with the chorus of insects. It was a time to explore the fields for new arrivals, observe the last of the snow melting into small ice patches, and watch small pools form, creating a delightful spot to float small wooden boats or other objects nearby.

Summer was a season of abundance. The brook swelled, inviting us to plunge into its refreshing depths and chase dragonflies that flitted like shimmering jewels. Farm work transitioned from safeguarding crops against the harsh winter and spring to preparing hay for the upcoming winter months. Occasionally, we would venture to a nearby lake, relishing the invigorating coolness of its water and the gentle waterfall at its edge. Each visit to the lake presented a novel adventure within the carefree embrace of summer.

Fall was akin to a grand spectacle. The leaves burst into fiery reds and golds, then danced down in slow, graceful spirals. Harvest time meant apple-picking, pumpkin-carving, and the sweet, smoky scent of wood smoke wafting through the trees. I recall the special moment we would pick the first apple from our orchard, holding it up like a trophy, savoring the crisp bite of autumn. However, who could resist tossing apples at a target from a distance? Perhaps a tree, a darting squirrel, or even a younger brother. Ah, those carefree days of wonder.

Winter concluded the season with a quiet hush. Snow covered everything, transforming the world into a soft, muted watercolor. The frozen pond became our playground for childhood adventures. Snowdrifts became a cozy spot to build a snow cave or an intriguing snowman.

Every season taught me something new about being flexible, thankful, and enjoying life's fleeting moments. Watching the leaves change was a gentle nudge that staying the same isn't real, and that fresh chances and new starts are always just around the corner.

As the Earth's timeless seasons unfold, so do our life cycles, each stage mirroring nature's rhythm. Childhood, like spring, is full of new beginnings and endless possibilities, where curiosity and innocence flourish. Youth, like summer, bursts with energy and passion, a time for exploration and youthful vigor. In maturity, we become autumn, grounded in experience and wisdom, sharing our knowledge and leaving a legacy. Old age, like winter, invites us to find peace in stillness and to reflect deeply, trusting in the completion of our journey. Life's balance of light and dark, growth and letting go, nurtures each phase, shaping us by our successes and losses. By nurturing new ideas in spring, enjoying summer's fruits, savoring autumn's richness, and resting in winter's calm, we learn that every stage, like every season, is vital to our existence.

Chapter Five

Spring

The Season of New Beginnings

Like a secret shared between earth and sky, spring emerged. The woods awoke in a symphony of green, tender shoots piercing the soil, buds swelling into blossoms, birds returning with songs I'd missed without realizing. The air smelled of wet earth and possibility. I remember kneeling to watch a ladybug climb a blade of grass, feeling as though I, too, was unfurling. Spring taught me renewal; how grief gives way to growth, how after every long, cold winter, warmth returns not just to the land but to the heart.

When we're born, we're so small and fragile. Like delicate shoots breaking through the soil, we need others to protect and feed us. But even in this early stage, we're growing. Every coo and cry is a way to connect; every hug plants seeds of trust. This season shows us that life starts not with strength, but with giving up—a gentle reminder that we're all born into a world that cares for us even before we know what we need.

As the snow melts and the earth warms up from the sun, the woods turn into a beautiful place of new beginnings. But soon, the forest bursts into color! Leaves open like pages in a book, and tiny flowers cling to branches, bursting into bloom as if the trees can't hold back any longer. After winter's long, hard sleep, the world starts to wake up in a quiet, beautiful way. It doesn't shout, but whispers: the first crocus pushing through the frost, robins returning to wet lawns, and snowmelt dripping from eaves turning into music. Spring doesn't just happen, it unfolds, one gentle moment at a time, like a letter slowly opened after a long silence.

The air is filled with possibilities. Birds sing a beautiful song, and the smell of wet soil and fresh growth fills the air with each step. Puddles are still on the trails, and streams are rushing with melted ice, but there's no time to remember the cold. Spring is a time to be in the moment, to be bold. Daffodils bow to the wind, and butterflies, as delicate as stained glass, flutter past.

Walking through the woods in spring feels like walking through a promise.

It reminds me that no matter how long winter lasts, life always comes back.

I feel it too, a longing inside me for growth, for letting go of the ice that's built up in my heart.

Spring shows that new life starts with a small act of bravery, and that light can break even the darkest times.

This season is more than just a change in temperature or daylight. It's not just what the calendar says. Spring is a living picture, a reminder etched into the earth's rhythms: no matter how frozen life feels, it's always possible to come back. Being still isn't a defeat. Being quiet isn't giving up. And every end—every harsh winter—holds the quiet promise of a new start.

The Joy of Release: Stepping Out of Winter's Shadow

Every spring, there's this magical moment when the earth breathes a sigh of relief, and life wakes up with a fresh sense of purpose, a feeling, not a clock or calendar. It happened when I opened the heavy barn door, its hinges creaking from months of stillness, and a cow cautiously stepped onto the dew-kissed grass for the first time in almost six months. Her coat, once smooth and shiny, is now matted from days spent in straw and shadow. Her breath, foggy in the crisp morning air, shows both hesitation and excitement. She sniffs the wind, green, damp, alive, and then, as if an ancient signal has only been heard in her heart, she leaps. Not a step, not a shuffle, but a full-bodied, hoof-kicking, tail-swishing leap into the wide-open morning. She trots in wide, clumsy circles, mooing not in sadness, but in joy, an unmistakable cry of freedom. It's a sound that doesn't need words to be felt. I am here. I am free. I am alive.

This simple, rural moment holds a truth that goes far beyond the pasture. It speaks to a universal human desire, for release, for renewal, for reconnecting with the world and with ourselves. Winter, in all its forms, has a way of trapping us. It isn't always measured in snow or frost-covered windows; sometimes, it lives in the quiet corners of our hearts, a season of emotional hibernation, of isolation, of postponed dreams.

We've all known winters that weren't on the calendar: periods of grief that slowed us down, seasons of burnout that dimmed our passions, relationships that turned cold and distant, or goals that slipped further into the fog with each passing month. Like the cow in the barn, we get comfortable in the confined space. We learn to move within narrow limits, to survive on limited light and stale air. We forget the feeling of the wind on our skin, the taste of possibility on our tongues.

But spring always makes its way in, doesn't it? It's not like it's pushing us; it's inviting us, soft, steady, and hard to resist. It shows up in the way the sun peeks over the horizon a bit longer, in a chat that stirs up an old dream, in a walk where your shoulders finally relax, or in that sudden urge to create, to move, to reach out. It's not about being perfect, but about being present. It's about stepping, not rushing, not leaping just yet, just stepping into the unknown with courage blooming like the first crocuses breaking through the thawing earth.

To step out of winter's shadow is to set free what held us captive. It's to let go of the stories we've clung to. I'm not ready. I'm not enough. It's too late. These are the frosty layers that built up quietly over time, fragile and beautiful in their familiarity, but ultimately suffocating. They were never truth, just survival strategies made in the cold. And now, like the cow finding her rhythm in the field, we too start to remember what movement feels like, not the tired shuffle of endurance, but the lively, unburdened dance of being fully alive.

The joy of letting go isn't just about feeling; it's about how our bodies and spirits respond. Science says sunlight boosts serotonin, movement releases endorphins, and connection fights cortisol, the stress hormone that builds up quietly when we're alone. But the wisdom of the pasture teaches us something older than numbers: that joy isn't a reward for having everything figured out. It's a natural reaction to freedom, a response to trading stagnation for space. When the cow kicks up her heels, she's not thinking about grazing patterns or milk production. She's simply enjoying the gift of the open field. And so, we must learn to respond, to welcome our own journey with wonder, not judgment.

Leaving the barn doesn't mean forgetting where we came from. It was a place that kept us safe through tough times. But safety and growth don't always go hand in hand. It's okay to remember where we've been and thank the walls that sheltered us, even as we step into the open. The important thing is to move with purpose, to notice the grass underfoot, to pause and breathe in the scent of the earth waking up. It's okay to be clumsy, uncertain, or even a little scared—real growth doesn't always happen smoothly at first.

So, what do we find in the field? Not just grass and sunshine, but a whole new world of possibilities.

We get to graze where we want, to touch a new flower, to wander or rest whenever we feel like it. In our lives, this means we get some time back, we can be creative again, our relationships can flourish, and projects we've put aside can come back to life. It's about having the courage to try something new, even if it feels a bit shaky. It's about rediscovering our curiosity, laughing at our mistakes instead of being too hard on ourselves, and letting hope return gently and steadily.

Just like a cow that, after a burst of energy, eventually slows down to graze quietly and contentedly, we too will find our new rhythm. But the memory of that leap, the pure, unfiltered joy of freedom, will stay with us. It becomes part of who we are. A reminder that we're not meant to be confined, no matter how long we've been. That our souls, like our bodies, need open skies and fresh air. That even after the longest winters, renewal is not only possible, but also inevitable, if we're willing to take that first, uncertain step.

So, let the gate swing open. Let the frost melt from your shoulders. Let your heart sink into the morning like a song only you can sing. The field is waiting. The grass is green. The sun is shining. And you—yes, you—are ready to dance.

The Sacred Work of Planting: Faith in What You Cannot Yet See

As the ground warms up, the farmer steps in, the gentle builder of new life. Even before the first green shoots peek through, they're out in the fields at dawn, guiding tractors through the softened earth. They're plowing, tilling, and getting everything ready. Each move is careful. Each furrow is a little prayer.

Planting is like putting your trust in something big. You scatter seeds into cold, dark soil, hoping they'll grow back. There might be storms, late frosts, bugs, and even moments of doubt. But you still plant.

Isn't that what it's all about?

To the Farmer Who Dances with the Dawn

When the first soft light of sunrise touches the horizon, you're already up, your silhouette a dark brushstroke against the morning's glow. The world is calm, just the gentle whisper of the wind through the wheat, already chatting with the sky. In these early moments, you stand at the edge of what could be, the keeper of a promise as old as the earth and as new as the seed you're about to bury in its warm embrace.

You're more than just a man or woman with calloused hands; you're the heart of life's gentle, steady beat. Every heartbeat you feel is like a metronome, guiding the plow, the seed, the row, and the harvest. The farm equipment you're now getting ready is like an orchestra of steel and rubber, each piece tuned to your touch. The engine's low rumble is a soft chant, a gentle reminder that before anything can grow, there needs to be space, a soft, open, and ready earth. I remember watching my dad change bearings in equipment, grease joints, weld extensions to the plow, and fix things that were resting over the winter but needed fixing before planting. If something breaks down when you're getting the soil ready and planting, it can waste precious time. As I got older, I started doing the same maintenance on equipment as my dad had done before. It's like getting our equipment ready for the planting season. Life is the same way: we need to live and appreciate it, to focus on the little things while also preparing for the unexpected.

The First Act: Plowing the Soil

You step onto the field, boots sinking a bit into the soil, feeling the earth's soft sigh beneath you. The tractor waits like a loyal horse, its shiny chrome catching the first light. You settle into the seat, hands resting on the wheel, and together you start the old conversation between man and earth.

The plow teeth, sharp as your determination, turn the earth over, pulling away the last bits of last season's work. Each furrow is a thought, a careful carving into the land's mind. You watch the dark, rich soil tumble, showing off the lighter, looser layers underneath, a canvas getting ready for the big picture. The plow's rhythm is a steady beat, and as the rows stretch out behind you, they become the veins through which future life will flow.

You know, a well-tilled field isn't just about getting the job done; it's a promise of respect. When you break up compacted earth, you're inviting oxygen to breathe, water to seep, and microorganisms to wake up. The soil, once a dense, stubborn mass, now yields a soft, crumbly texture that cradles possibility. In each turned clod, you sense the quiet gratitude of the ground, acknowledging that you've honored its need for renewal.

As a young teen, I spent hours on the tractor plowing the field, trying to keep straight rows so that my dad wouldn't comment on my lack of attention to detail. There was satisfaction at the end of the day, looking across the plowed field, knowing this was part of a bigger plan.

Selecting the Right Seeds: A Covenant of Choice

Now that the field is all set, it's time to pick the seeds that will really make your farm shine! This part feels like a sacred moment. You're going through bags of kernels, each one like a tiny treasure chest of genetic stories, a whisper from fields far away and generations of breeders.

Corn, that golden giant, is a picture in your mind. Each kernel is like a little sun, promising not just lots of grain, but also strong stalks that sway in the breeze, giving birds a place to rest and showing off how hot the summer was. You pick a hybrid that can handle dry spells, one with roots that dig deep to find hidden water, a kind that can grow even when it doesn't rain. I remember listening to my dad talk about how different hybrid seeds work, often sharing stories from his childhood and experiments with his dad to find the best mix that could fight off bugs.

Oats, the simple yet tough grain, call to you with their silvery spikes. Their neat, even growth gives off a different kind of beauty, a tidy, consistent pattern that speaks of reliability and nourishment. You pick a variety that grows early, ready to feed everyone before the corn even gets tall.

You don't just pick seeds without thinking. You check the weather, look at the soil, and see what's happening in the market. You think about how the past seasons have been—how a late frost once ruined a hopeful crop, or how a big oat harvest fed everyone and the animals. In this careful thinking, you feel both the responsibility and the thrill of caring for your farm. Each seed you save is a promise to take care of it, protect it, and trust the earth to give you back what you give it.

Fertilizer: The Quiet Blending of Science with Nature

Between the soil and the seed, there's a third player, fertilizer. It's not just a chemical mix; it's a carefully crafted blend that helps the earth share its hidden bounty. You look at the soil test results, the pH, and the levels of nitrogen, phosphorus, and potassium, and then you map out what the field needs on your mental map.

You choose a balanced mix that will give the natural nutrients a boost without overwhelming the tiny, helpful microbes you've nurtured with your plowing. You measure each bag with the precision of a scientist, but with the heart of a poet, knowing that too much could harm the roots, while too little would leave the seedlings hungry. It's a dance of numbers and intuition, a balancing act that shows the harmony you're aiming for.

You spread the fertilizer in a thin, even layer, letting it settle gently into the furrows. As you do, you whisper a quiet hope that this nourishment will be taken up by the roots, transformed by the soil's unseen hands, and delivered to the shoots that will soon push through the surface.

When I was a kid, I trusted my dad to figure out the right mix and just applied the fertilizer to the fields based on what he thought.

Sometimes, we need to follow the lead of others who've already walked the path before us, even if we think we know the way.

Planting: Rows of Dreams, Patterns of Purpose

Now, the ground finally meets the future. You climb onto the tractor, confident in starting the planting ritual, each seed placed with an intention that goes beyond just planting.

Corn in Distinct Rows

You plant the corn seeds at regular intervals, spacing each kernel just enough to give its future stalk room to reach for the sky. The rows become bold, straight lines that cut through the field like verses of a poem, each line a stanza promising height, strength, and a golden harvest. As you plant each seed in the soil, you imagine it pushing up through the ground, how it will become a mature corn stalk in a sea across a full field.

I remember as a teen, planting corn with the tractor and two-row planter, thinking I was doing something meaningful. As I drove the tractor, I started dreaming about other things and didn't pay attention to keeping the rows straight. Of course, nobody noticed that I didn't plant the seeds in a straight row until the fruits of the planting were revealed. By then, it was too late to make any corrections. This is a greater lesson for life.

If we stop paying attention to details, we may not know the impact until it's too late to make a change.

Oats in Uniform Pattern

You turn to the oats, arranging them in a careful, even pattern. Their seeds are packed together, creating a thick mat that, once they sprout, will become a beautiful, silvery sea. The neatness isn't just for looks; it's a smart way to use the oats' natural tendency to spread and take over, making sure the plants are evenly spaced and strong enough to fight off weeds and give you the best possible harvest. The way you lay them out feels like a chessboard—each piece placed with thought, each move designed to protect the kingdom you're building.

As you work, you keep a mental tally, figuring out just how much seed to put in each acre, how deep to plant it, and how far apart to space them. These numbers are all about being efficient and caring for the land. You double-check your calculations, knowing that a mistake could cost not just money, but also the livelihoods of the community that depends on your harvest.

The Quiet Anticipation

When the last seed is tucked into its little home in the earth, you step back and look at what you've done. The rows of corn stand like disciplined soldiers ready for action, while the oats form a soft, peaceful carpet, all set to grow together. The field now looks like a living map, a promise written into the land, waiting to bloom.

In the days that follow, you'll watch the seedlings push through the soil, their first green leaves unfurling, and reach for the sun. You'll help them by pulling out weeds that try to choke them and by keeping an eye out for pests that might eat them, making sure they have a good chance to grow and give you a great harvest. You'll measure how they're growing, see how they compare to what you thought they would be, and adjust how you take care of them.

There's a little worry in your stomach, a soft voice saying, "Will this be enough?" But inside that worry, there's a strong, unwavering hope. The same hope that inspired your ancestors to farm, that led them to write the first farming books, and that still has the same strength today.

It's this hope that keeps the farmer going, turning hard work into love and turning sweat into success. The same hope we have when we put in the preparation work that turns our efforts into success.

The Harvest's Promise

When the time comes to harvest, the fields will shine as a testament to your hard work. The corn will grow tall and golden, each ear packed with sweetness that will feed families, livestock, and maybe even reach far-off markets. The oats will sparkle, their grains ready to be ground into warm porridge, used in breads, or fed to animals that will, in turn, nurture the next generation.

But there's more than just the physical harvest; there's a deeper one: a harvest of character, perseverance, and a renewed bond between people and the earth each season. With careful planning, thoughtful choices, and patient waiting, you can coax life from the soil, hope from the sky, and joy from the act of nurturing.

To the farmer who turns earth into promise, may every seed you sow return to you tenfold.

Chapter Six

Summer

The Bloom of Curiosity

By summer, the woods pulsed with life. Sunlight filtered through a canopy so dense it painted the forest floor in emerald mosaics. I'd lie on my back, counting leaves instead of stars, listening to cicadas hum their midday hymns. Fireflies danced at twilight, and the scent of pine clung to my clothes. This was abundance, bold, bright, unafraid. Summer taught me joy, not as an escape, but as a celebration of being alive. It reminded me to soak in the moment, for even the brightest days pass swiftly.

Childhood is a burst of color, just like summer's joy. It's the time when we're wide-eyed and curious, always asking "why" and "how," our minds stretching out like vines reaching for the sun. Falls and scrapes become lessons in strength; laughter and tears mix as we learn about friends and our imaginations. It's a time to explore, when the world feels endless, and mistakes are just steps forward, not failures. Here, we learn that growing up isn't a straight line but a spiral—a dance of discovery that shapes who we are and what we dream of.

There's a magical moment in the heart of summer when everything seems to pause and breathe. The wild energy of spring, with its bursts of growth and hurried preparations, fades into a gentle, flowing rhythm. The forest, now a vibrant tapestry of green, invites you to slow down, linger, and soak in its abundance. Summer isn't about scarcity; it's a beautiful symphony of giving, a time when the earth opens its arms wide and shares its treasures with those who pause, look closely, and accept. It's a season that teaches us to be present, to savor, and to appreciate the simple joys of life. In its golden light, we find a reminder that the most profound happiness is found right here, in the present moment, not in distant dreams.

The Forest as a Sanctuary

By midsummer, the forest becomes a cathedral of light and life. The canopy thickens, its emerald leaves creating a living roof that filters sunlight into beautiful patterns on the forest floor. Golden beams pierce through the branches, lighting up the mossy ground like a painter's brushstroke. The air is warm and alive, not heavy or stifling, but a gentle embrace that carries the scent of pine resin, damp earth, and the sweet aroma of ripening fruit.

Stepping beneath this lush archway is like entering a sanctuary. The world outside feels far away here.

In the woods of summer, time seems to melt away. Instead of counting moments, you start to experience them: the way sunlight dances on a spiderweb, how the breeze whispers leaves into a gentle rustling, the sudden stillness before a deer cautiously steps out from the underbrush. This is a place where the heart calms, and the soul remembers how to breathe deeply.

The Abundance of Nature's Table

Summer is all about abundance, more sunshine, more growth, and more vibrant colors. The forest floor is a lively scene: ferns unfurl like green fireworks, wildflowers sway in clusters of violet, gold, and crimson, and branches heavy with fruit. Blackberries, their skins glistening like ink, raspberries as crimson as summer sunsets, and wild strawberries, tiny and jewel-like, each offers a burst of sweetness to those brave enough to handle the thorns.

Nature is a generous host, and summer is its feast. It invites us to pick a plum from the tree, sip water from a moss-cupped pool, and let the earth's gifts nourish you. This abundance is not just passive; it's a language. The season's prolific offerings whisper truths about generosity and reciprocity. When the earth shares so freely, what might we choose to share in return? What parts of ourselves, our time, our care, our creativity, might we give to the world, trusting that it will echo our generosity back to us?

A Tapestry of Connection

Summer is alive with life, and every creature has a part to play in the dance. Squirrels dart up trunks, their bushy tails flicking like brushes of sunlight. Dragonflies, jewel-toned and fleeting, skim the surface of ponds, their iridescent wings catching the light like stained glass. High above, the solemn hoot of an owl reminds us that even in the brightest days, mystery lingers.

Wandering through the woods in summer feels like stepping into a living tapestry of connections.

Imagine a squirrel burying acorns, setting the stage for future forests; a beaver building a pond that becomes a sanctuary for frogs and herons, or a pollinator flitting from flower to flower, ensuring countless species thrive. These interactions aren't just random; they're a beautiful reminder of how everything is interconnected and how life depends on one another. And guess what? We're all part of this story too. When we sit quietly by a stream, listening to the gentle flow of water and the cheerful songs of birds, we're reminded that we're not separate from this world but deeply connected to it.

The Art of Slowing Down

Summer's gentle pace has a special kind of magic. It encourages us to let go of the idea that we have to be constantly productive and instead focus on being present. I remember spending a lazy afternoon wading through a sunlit stream, my feet sinking into the cool, pebbled water. The water was like a mirror, showing the clouds drifting by, and for a moment, I completely forgot about my worries. I was just there, part of the sky, the water, the ancient heartbeat of the earth.

Summer teaches us that stillness isn't empty; it's full. It's in these quiet moments that we often discover the unexpected: a fox quietly walking through the meadow, the first fireflies of the season twinkling like stars come down to earth, or the gentle opening of our hearts when we let them soften.

Of course, summer also celebrates movement. There's energy in exploring, the excitement of hiking a sun-dappled trail, the laughter of friends around a bonfire, or the sweat on your brow as you dig in the garden. Summer is the dance that combines activity and rest, reminding us that true vitality comes from balance, knowing when to move and when to pause.

A Playground of Light, Speed, and Unbound Imagination

When the days are long and the air is filled with the gentle, warm hum of cicadas, the old barn transforms from just a pile of weathered beams and rust-spotted metal roofs into a stage for some of the simplest, yet wonderfully freeing, summer rituals. It's the rhythmic bounce of a sponge ball against its worn side, the thrilling slide of a four-wheel, metal-rimmed cart down its gentle slopes, and the quiet, almost reverent, appreciation of an open sky that invites your mind to wander far beyond the fence line. Maybe even trying to launch a model rocket from the gravel path to the barn. In the quiet of these simple actions, a child (or the child within us) discovers a timeless truth: freedom isn't a place we reach; it's a feeling we create in the moments when we let the world and our imagination guide the way.

The Sponge Ball's Echo: A Beat of Summer's Heart

There's a special magic in the sound of a sponge ball hitting the barn's wooden side. It starts with a soft "thwap," a gentle, pliable impact that echoes through the loft's rafters and into the open field. Each bounce sends a wave of vibration through the dry boards, turning the structure into a living drum. I looked forward to each bounce as it ricocheted off the rough barn wall in different directions. With a ball glove in hand, I was a left-hander using a right-hander's ball glove, trying to catch each rebound.

The ball, though simple, is a true hero. Its soft surface absorbs the July sun, swelling slightly as it warms, and then it bounces back with a gentle, forgiving bounce. Unlike a hard rubber ball that might bounce away in a chaotic spray, the sponge ball gives you a steady, almost calming rhythm. With each hit, it slides a few inches along the barn's side before bouncing back into your hand, where you adjust your stance and keep going. At times, I would throw the ball on the barn roof, anticipating where it would roll back as I tried to catch it. This repetitive motion becomes a mantra: breathe in, strike, watch the ball's arc, breathe out. In this quiet focus, your mind clears, and you become aware of a subtle connection between your body, the object, and your surroundings.

Beyond the physical sensations, this simple game teaches us something deeper.

The sponge ball's soft bounce reminds us that strength doesn't always have to be hard or aggressive; resilience can be flexible, adaptable, and gentle. It teaches us to find joy in the small things, to celebrate the ordinary, and to turn the barn's plain walls into a canvas for kinetic poetry.

The Metal-Rimmed Cart: A Four-Wheel Voyage into Freedom

If the sponge ball gives you a pulse, the four-wheel, metal-rimmed cart gives you speed. Made from old wood and steel-rimmed wagon wheels, the cart's frame shines in the summer sun, with its rims catching a rainbow of light. When I get on, sitting on the edge of its worn wooden seat, the barn's gravel ramp, once a path for feed wagons, becomes a launchpad for your imagination.

The ride down the ramp is like a magical dance between physics and imagination. Gravity is the star, gently pulling the cart forward with a steady, unstoppable pull. The metal rims spin, creating a soft, metallic whir that blends beautifully with the rustling hay and the distant hoot of a barn owl starting its night song. Once I was comfortable with the short trips down the barn ramp, I thought, "Why not take the cart to the top of a hill beyond the house?" As the cart speeds down, the world turns into streaks of green grass, sun-dappled dust, and the occasional butterfly fluttering by.

In those quick moments, I felt a wonderful mix of being in control and letting go. My hands hold onto the old wooden handles, knuckles white with excitement, while my body leans forward, trusting the cart to be strong. It's like flying, but still on the ground, freeing my mind from grown-up worries and letting it wander as far as the wind takes me.

The cart isn't just for fun; it's a way to tell stories. Kids picture themselves as explorers, racing in a big competition, or daring to discover new places. The ramp becomes a mountain, the barn's open doors a way to faraway lands, and the cart, a trusty steed, carries them across the limits of what's real. In this simple ride, the summer landscape becomes a stage for endless stories.

When the Moon Becomes a Mirror for the Mind

I often think of the night sky as a silent cinema, showing its own stories to those who gaze up. Watching the Moon, with its gentle, unblinking gaze and its half-hidden presence over the world, fills me with a special kind of awe. It's like a beacon for anyone who's ever wondered what's beyond our atmosphere. For me, each time the Moon rose, thin and silver on a velvet sky, it felt like a personal journey back to the summer of 1969, when Neil

Armstrong and Buzz Aldrin first touched its powdery surface.

I remember the exact moment it happened in my neighbor's living room: a warm July evening, fireflies twinkling like little lanterns, and the distant rumble of a TV broadcasting the historic footage. The camera shifted from the huge, sparkling astronaut helmets to the grainy, black-and-white images of the lunar surface. It felt like the world held its breath; a collective gasp rose from every corner of Earth as those two men, still men, still boys in the eyes of a child, took those first steps. "One small step for man, one giant leap for mankind," Neil said, and those words seemed to fall like soft meteors onto my imagination, landing with a certainty that shook my very being.

It hit me like a bolt of lightning: What if the Moon could be more than just a distant rock? What if it could be a place waiting for an ordinary kid with a cardboard box and a few pieces of duct tape? I felt a pull, an invisible tether, a rope that seemed to connect my heart to that glowing sphere. It was made of curiosity, courage, and a tiny, stubborn spark of imagination.

That night, I wasn't just gazing at a star; I felt a spark of possibility. The bright silver disc seemed like a blank canvas, waiting for my own stories to unfold. I pictured rockets, sleek, silver arrows slicing through the night, leaving a trail of starlight in their wake. I imagined those rockets carrying not just metal and fuel, but the dreams of every child who has ever gazed up, wondered, and whispered, "What if?" I knew the idea was far-fetched. What child could ever imagine their backyard toy could bridge the gap between Earth and the Moon? Yet, dreaming stretched my imagination, and that stretch made everything so magical.

I decided to build my own rocket. I spent an entire afternoon at the workbench, my hands shaking not from the glue but from the electric excitement coursing through me. I remember the smell of fresh paint. Each piece I attached felt like a promise, a tiny vow to the universe that I wouldn't just watch the Moon; I would aim to touch it, even if it was just in spirit.

Then came the first launch. I set the rocket on a small, homemade launch pad, placed on the gravel in front of the barn. It looked so small compared to the huge, imagined catapults of NASA. My heart pounded as I counted down: "Three... two... one...." The ignition crackled, a sudden flash of orange that briefly lit up the evening shadows. The rocket shot up, carving a thin line across the dusk sky before disappearing into the deepening blue.

For a fleeting moment, it felt like a tiny piece of the Moon had broken free from Earth, a reminder of humanity's journey to that distant world. I cheered, my voice cracking with pure excitement, feeling a deep connection to the astronauts who had walked on the Moon just months before. My model rocket couldn't carry a man, hold a flag, or leave footprints, but it carried something even more valuable: belief. It reminded me that the line between imagination and reality is often a thin, invisible barrier that can be broken with enough determination, curiosity, and a touch of boldness.

In the days that followed, each new launch was like an experiment, a leap of faith, and a moment of reflection. Some rockets veered off course, spiraling into the grass like confused fireflies. Others struggled and sputtered, never quite catching the flame they were supposed to. Each failure threatened to dim the glow of my lunar dreams, but each attempt also taught me something about the power of dreaming. I began to realize that imagination isn't just a single, fixed picture of what could be; it's a dynamic process, constantly changing with each success, each failure, and each quiet moment of thought under the Moon's watchful eye.

There were evenings when I would sit on the porch steps, gaze at the Moon, and let my mind wander to the days when rockets the size of houses roared out of launch pads, carrying brave souls beyond the atmosphere. My model rockets, though small, became tiny symbols of the same longing that drove Apollo 11. In those moments, I felt a sense of connection with the engineers and scientists who had turned a dream into reality. They all started with a simple act: looking up at the Moon and daring to imagine.

Some might think it was a bit far-fetched, maybe even too far, to imagine that a homemade rocket could ever get us to the Moon. But that very idea is what makes us wonder. It's our minds' ability to stretch and imagine beyond what we can do now, into what we can do tomorrow. Inside every child's heart, there's a slingshot pointing at the stars. The rocket is just the rubber band that holds all the energy of hope, waiting for the right moment to let go.

Years later, when I was sitting in a college classroom, listening to professors talk about how things move in space and how rockets work, I could still remember those simple evenings so clearly. The equations on the blackboard weren't just abstract symbols; they were the language that had once turned my childlike wonder into a real, if small, craft that could zoom through the air. The ideas of thrust, drag, and where the rocket would go weren't just stuff for books; they were the whispers of the winds that had taken my imagination from the porch to the stars.

Even now, as an adult who's retired from NASA and sometimes feels a bit removed from the simple act of sticking plastic fins on a rocket, I still find myself going back to that Moonlit porch. When doubts pop up, when deadlines are coming, and the world feels heavy, I step outside, look up, and let the Moon be my guide. I remember that the same celestial body that saw Armstrong's big step also saw a kid's serious attempt to send a tiny craft into the sky. The Moon, calm and always there, reminds me that it doesn't care if the traveler is an astronaut in a big suit or a teenager with a homemade rocket; it only cares that the traveler dares to look up.

The lesson I've learned is straightforward and deep: imagination doesn't have to be big or small. It can be as big as a mission to another planet or as small as a launch in your backyard. It's what keeps us going, the hidden force that pushes us toward our own personal goals. And when the night sky is clear, the Moon is low, and almost close, I remember that my imagination is not just about what I've seen, but what I've dared to imagine.

So, the next time you look up at that bright disc, don't just watch it. Let it inspire you—a reminder that when we focus on a simple, shining rock in the sky, we can launch rockets, both real and in our minds, that go way beyond what we think we can do. Our minds can really wonder, and that wonder is what makes a child's backyard model a symbol of how far we can reach. The Moon isn't just a faraway place; it's a mirror showing us the huge, unexplored parts of our own imagination. And every time we look at it, we're invited to build, launch, and keep dreaming—one small step at a time, toward our own big leaps.

The Landscape: A Living Canvas for Imagination

The sponge ball, cart, and model rockets are tangible things, but what really makes this summer scene special is the environment. The barn, with its cracked siding, rusty tin roof, and creaking loft doors, isn't just a backdrop; it's a character in its own right. Sunlight dances through the roof's gaps, casting shifting patterns on the floorboards. The smell of fresh hay, mixed with the subtle fragrance of wildflowers that have wandered from the meadow, weaves a sense that stirs memories and sparks daydreams.

The sky above is a perfect, endless blue, dotted with fluffy clouds that drift lazily across the horizon. Its vastness invites us to dream: each cloud can be a ship, a dragon, or a castle in the sky, while the line where earth meets sky whispers of adventures waiting to be found. The warm, but never stifling, temperature invites our skin to bask in the gentle sun, a reminder that nature's touch can be both soothing and invigorating.

Even the sounds of summer, crickets singing in the late afternoon, the soft hum of distant tractors, and the occasional bark of a farm dog, add a rhythm to the day. They become the music for a child's inner world, a steady beat that supports the creative dance of imagination. The world feels bigger, yet more connected; there's a strange sense of belonging to something grand while being held safe by the familiar barnyard.

The Freedom to Imagine: An Inner Landscape Unfolds

What really sets a summer at the barn apart from a regular afternoon is the freedom that blooms in our minds. When a child gets a sponge ball, a sturdy cart, or a model rocket, the tools are simple, but the possibilities they unlock are endless.

This freedom isn't about not having rules, but about being allowed to think without limits, to explore without fear, and to create stories that go beyond what's physically possible.

Think of imagination as a muscle, right? Just like when I bounced a sponge ball, each bounce helped my mind get better at spotting tiny changes, like how the ball moves or how the sound echoes. This sharpened my observational skills, making me more aware in everyday life. Every time I zoomed down the ramp or launched a rocket, it built my confidence, and I learned that taking risks can lead to rewards. Together, these experiences reinforce the idea that the world is a playground, and we're all eager to play.

Plus, this freedom is shared. Often, friends gather around the barn, taking turns with the ball, cheering each other on as they zoom down the ramp, and sharing stories of their imagined adventures. The bonds you form in those moments teach you to be empathetic, work together, and enjoy shared successes. The barn becomes a place where memories are made—where laughter is carved into the wood, where scratches on the cart's rim tell stories of many rides, and where a dent in the sponge ball marks a particularly exciting game.

Lessons That Stick Around

Even when the leaves turn golden and the days get shorter, the barn's doors close for a while, but the memories of those summer days stay with you. The skills I learned, like being resilient, imaginative, confident, and working together, don't just stay with me as a kid; as I grew up, these lessons helped me handle challenges, build relationships, and find joy in the little things.

As an adult who spent summers bouncing sponge balls, when I'm at a desk and facing a tough decision, I remember how much patience it takes to watch a ball's path and try to carry that patience into my own decision-making. The memory of racing down a ramp or launching a model rocket gives me the courage to take calculated risks. And the respect I have for the open sky might make me appreciate moments of peace in a busy life, reminding me to pause and breathe.

The barn's simple summer rituals become metaphors for life's bigger journey. The sponge ball's thwap reminds us that every action has a ripple effect. The cart's quick slide shows that once we start moving, we can keep going if we trust the path. And the sky, always there, reminds us that there are endless possibilities if we just look up and dream.

Embracing the Summer Within

Even if you've never been to a barn, you can recreate the feeling anywhere, on a city rooftop, in a quiet park, or even in your living room with a ramp and a soft ball. The key is to have something to play with, a space to move around, and the courage to let your imagination lead the way.

Take a moment today to find your own "barn." Maybe it's a cozy spot where you can bounce a tennis ball against a wall and listen to its sound. Maybe it's a sturdy chair you can push across a smooth floor, feeling the rush of a simple glide. Or maybe it's a small wooden cart you can roll down a gentle hill in a garden. As you play with these things, notice how your mind wanders, how stories come to life, and how a sense of freedom fills your heart. Let yourself enjoy being fully present, feeling the sun on your skin, the wind in your hair, and the gentle hum of life around you.

By doing this, you're celebrating the timeless spirit of summer at the barn, a spirit that reminds us that, no matter how old we are or what we're doing, we can always find the joy of a sponge ball's bounce, the thrill of a cart's slide, and the endless sky above. The world is waiting, ready to echo with your imagination, if you just dare to listen.

Savoring the Moment: Summer's Greatest Lesson

Summer's greatest gift is its gentle nudge to slow down and truly enjoy life. It's about savoring every moment, letting your senses soak in the world without rushing through it. Imagine feeling the sun's warmth on your skin, tasting the burst of flavor in a freshly picked berry, or listening to the soothing sound of rain on leaves.

In our fast-paced world, where "busyness" often feels like purpose, summer is a gentle reminder to pause. It encourages us to look, breathe, and simply be. It reminds us that joy isn't something we chase but a state of being, a quiet, sunlit presence that blooms when we stop and notice.

I remember one evening, camping in the woods, when the air cooled, and the first stars appeared in the deep blue sky. The water nearby sparkled with the moon's silver light, and crickets sang like a hymn. In that moment, I felt the full experience of being alive—the beauty and fragility, the fleeting and the eternal. And I realized that summer, with all its abundance, is a teacher. It shows us that we can also bloom when we turn toward the light, when we trust in the ripeness of this moment.

Carrying Summer's Abundance Forward

As summer winds down, its lessons stay with us. The forest thins, and the light changes, turning golden and honeyed, but the echoes of abundance remain. We carry them in the seeds we gathered, in the memories of laughter around a fire, and in the quiet wisdom of the season that taught us to be fully present.

> *Summer reminds us that we're part of the earth's rhythm, a season of growth, generosity, and connection. It challenges us to ask: How can we live with more abundance in our hearts, not just in summer but in all seasons? How can we honor the present, savor it as the forest savors the light, and give freely as the earth gives to us?*

So, as you wander through the last weeks of summer, let it stir your soul. Bask in its warmth, dance in its showers, and listen closely to its whispers. For in this season of abundance, we find a reflection of ourselves, reminders that we can bloom, give, and glow.

Chapter Seven

Autumn

The Harvest of Purpose

In late September or early October, or maybe it's just your luck, the world seems to pause. The air gets crisp, the light softens, and the trees, in a silent agreement, burst into a golden, crimson, and amber glow. It's autumn's grand entrance, a season that arrives with a bang, as if the earth is putting on one last, dazzling show before winter takes over. This is the Farewell Waltz of the year, a time to learn how to let go with grace and find beauty in giving up.

The trees were ablaze with gold and crimson, leaves swirling like embers in the wind. The air turned crisp, filled with the scent of decay and ripeness: the sweet rot of apples left behind under the trees, the earthy musk of mushrooms in the underbrush. I'd gather acorns, stack them like treasures, knowing they held the promise of forests yet to come. Autumn taught me the beauty of letting go. It showed me that releasing something doesn't mean losing it; it's a transformation, a way for something new to begin.

Adulthood comes with the crispness of autumn, a time of plenty and letting go. We start taking on responsibilities: jobs, relationships, families. Like trees heavy with fruit, we give of ourselves, often quietly, to care for those we love. But this season also brings change—old habits, fears, or dreams we've put off might fall away, making room for clarity. It's a time to balance what we need to do with what we love, to find happiness in small acts of kindness, and to realize that our purpose often comes from doing what matters every day.

Autumn isn't about having less; it's about letting go. The trees, once lush and green, gently release the leaves that have been their friends through spring's renewal and summer's bounty. There's no fuss in this letting go, no clinging to what was. The leaves fall not as if they're dying, but as happy participants in a cycle they've known for ages. They drift down like whispered secrets, creating a beautiful mix of decay and shine under our feet.

I often wonder what stories those leaves have. Did they shelter nests, catch rain from spring, or maybe even be the stage for a child's happy memories? Each one has done its job, and now, with the changing light, they return to the earth, not in a rush, but with thanks. Autumn reminds us that everything has its time, and letting go isn't a sign of weakness or loss, but a way of trusting life's natural flow.

The Beauty of Impermanence

The Japanese idea of *mono no aware*, that bittersweet feeling of knowing life is fleeting, really captures the spirit of autumn. It stirs a familiar ache in your heart when you see a maple leaf gently fall, or a tear in your eye when you realize this is the last walk through the woods before spring arrives. But there's also a sense of joy in it all: the thrill of a red leaf floating in the air, like a flickering flame before it lands; the laughter of kids jumping into piles of leaves, completely unaware of the coming cold; and the comforting hug of a woolen scarf and a warm mug of cider. Autumn's beauty goes beyond just acknowledging our mortality; it's about celebrating those fleeting moments that make life so special.

This season encourages us to think about what we hold onto. What are the "leaves" we're clinging to, old grudges, dreams that don't work anymore, relationships that have run their course? Autumn doesn't mourn the loss of its leaves; it embraces them, celebrates them. So, why do we hesitate to let go of what no longer helps us? The trees don't hold onto their leaves out of fear of being empty. They know that by letting go, they make room for new growth. The forest doesn't feel sad about its bare branches; it stands strong in its vulnerability, proud of its bravery to let go. There's a quiet confidence in the bare oak, a dignity in the skeletal remains of the birch. Even as the world slows down, there's a stillness that speaks of getting ready, resting, dreaming in the dark. Surrender isn't about giving up. It's about being true to what is, not what we wish it were. Autumn teaches this lesson in every rustling leaf: that we can't control the seasons or the changes inside ourselves. But we can choose how we deal with them. We can fall gracefully, like the leaves, or hold on too tight to our branches until the wind tears us apart. The season invites us to trust the ground beneath us, to know that even when we let go, we're still supported. One of autumn's most interesting things is how it's both about letting go and being beautiful.

Autumn's Invitation to Transformation

Isn't a fallen leaf just a seed waiting to transform? As leaves decompose, they return to the soil, giving roots the nutrients they need to grow new life. The forest floor becomes a place where new life can take root, showing us that endings aren't the end, but just the beginning. Autumn reminds us that every goodbye can lead to something new.

How can we bring this idea into our own lives? Maybe by letting go of the need to control everything and trusting that change is a natural part of life. It could be as easy as forgiving a mistake, dreaming big again, or stepping away from something that no longer feels right. Autumn teaches us that even the most beautiful leaves need to fall before they can become something new.

The Eternal Dance

No stage is ever truly alone. Each stage builds on the last, forming a continuous loop where endings open doors to new starts. The wisdom gained in the winter was developed in the spring, nurtured in the summer, and gathered in the autumn. So, let's welcome each phase with bravery, knowing that growth isn't just for the young; it's a lasting tune that plays on throughout our lives.

As we start our journey, pause for a moment to enjoy the season. Whether you're just starting out, growing and learning, staying true to yourself, or showing signs of maturity, you're exactly where you need to be, surrounded by the beauty of change. We don't know what the future holds, and we can't promise anything. Make each day count. Just like nature's seasons, life's seasons can bring sadness or give us a chance to think.

Chapter Eight

Winter

The Stillness of Wisdom

Winter came first in my memories, crisp, hushed, and silver. The world was wrapped in silence, blanketed by snow that muffled every footfall. I crunched through frost-laced paths, breath curling in the air like ghostly ribbons. Bare branches reached skyward like frozen prayers, yet even in stillness, there was strength. Winter taught me resilience, the beauty of rest, of enduring, of waiting with dignity. It whispered that even in dormancy, life pulses beneath the surface, gathering strength for what's to come.

As we get older, things slow down, and the world whispers its final lessons. Winter isn't an end, but a pause, a chance to think about a life well-lived. The body might feel tired, but the mind, like old wood, holds the stories of many years. This season invites us to face our own fragility, yes, but also to find peace in knowing we've loved, worked hard, and made a difference in the world. It's in winter that we learn the most important truth: life is short, so let's cherish every moment.

There's a special stillness in the woods during winter. The world seems to pause, wrapped in a blanket of snow that muffles all sounds. The only rhythm is my footsteps, a steady heartbeat against the quiet woods. The air is crisp and clean, yet it carries a strange peace. Trees, stripped of their leaves, show their true selves, gnarly and weathered, yet strong. They stand as proof of endurance, their icy branches shaped by the wind into delicate, crystalline works of art.

Winter isn't empty; it's full. Full of quiet strength. When I walk in this season, I feel a pull to slow down, to listen. The absence of color and movement becomes a canvas for my imagination. I notice the tracks of a fox slipping through the snow, the way icicles hang like nature's chandeliers, and the way the sun, though pale, makes the frost sparkle like scattered diamonds. Winter teaches me that rest isn't just doing nothing, and stillness isn't just being still. It's a season for reflection, for dreaming beneath layers of wool and hope.

In the forest's quiet, I find the courage to face my own quietness; even when things are dormant, there's purpose. Beneath the frozen ground, roots are working, getting ready for the rebirth that's coming.

Winter has this amazing way of turning everything into a peaceful, snowy paradise. As the first snowflakes begin to fall, they form beautiful patterns that cover the ground, turning ordinary places into pure white wonderlands. Snow drifts gently along fences and tree lines, whispering stories of the season's quiet magic. There's a calm that settles over everything, a pause in life that invites us to slow down and enjoy the stillness. In this season of frost and frost-kissed beauty, nature shows us how strong, unique, and joyful it is to get ready. I look at winter's wonders and see what it teaches us about living with grace and gratitude.

The Dance of Snowflakes: Embracing Individuality

There's a special magic in winter's first snowfall and the stillness that covers the world, the soft and gentle fall of countless snowflakes from the sky. Each tiny crystal spirals down like a secret whispered from the heavens, different in shape, created by the invisible magic of cold air and water. No two are the same, so they say, and after hours of looking through a magnifying glass, chasing flakes on black velvet to prove it, I can tell you: it's true. Not one pair matched. Not a single twin among the ones I saw.

Snowflakes have fascinated people for ages. One of those people was [1] Wilson A Bentley: Pioneering Photographer of Snowflakes. Wilson Bentley, a simple farmer from Vermont in the 1800s, who loved snowflakes so much that he changed how we see winter's most delicate gifts. With a microscope and a camera he borrowed, he became the first to take a picture of a single snowflake in 1885. Over his life, he took over 5,000 pictures—each one a surprise. Bentley once said, "Under the microscope, I saw that snowflakes were masterpieces of design." That phrase has stuck with me ever since I first heard it. Masterpieces. Not mistakes. Not random ice. Beautiful, special works of art.

When you look at snow from afar, it seems like it's all the same, white, soft, and smooth. It covers everything, like fields and rooftops, making everything blend together. You wouldn't know that underneath all that beauty, there's a whole world of

---

1. Smithsonian Institute Archives

uniqueness. Each flake has its own story shaped by temperature changes, wind, and tiny particles in the air, so no two are exactly alike.

Seems like we're in a world that often wants us to blend in. We're influenced to wear the same clothes, say the same things, and follow the same path. From school to work, it feels like we're always being asked to fit in. Be efficient. Be predictable. Be like everyone else. But nature, with her quiet wisdom, shows us something much deeper: that real beauty comes from being different. Try wearing a Steelers tie or jersey in the middle of Ravens' football country. Maybe that's a bit much, but take the time to be yourself. I remember once in high school wearing a wooden clog on one foot and a regular slip-on on the other. I probably could have found a more comfortable shoe, but it was different. That's not always the difference I'm talking about, but maybe it is.

Just as no two snowflakes are alike, no two people are either. Our fingerprints, DNA, and life stories are all unique. How often do we keep our true selves hidden to avoid being different? Do we keep our quirks to ourselves, like that strange hobby, that wild dream, or the way we laugh or cry, because they don't fit in?

Winter reminds us to embrace our unique qualities. It encourages us to let our individuality gently fall onto the world, like snow. After all, a snowstorm isn't beautiful since it's the same everywhere; it's beautiful because it's full of different shapes and sizes. The same is true of people.

I remember standing outside one winter evening, holding out my gloved hand as snow fell. I watched one flake land, sparkling under the porch light, its arms spreading out in perfect symmetry, each branch covered with tiny, crystal-like branches. It only lasted a few seconds before melting into a tiny drop of water. It was gone too soon. It was just a moment. But for that brief time, it was perfect. It was completely itself.

Isn't that what we all are? We're fleeting, yes, but we shine in our own way. We don't need to last forever to matter. We don't need to be exactly like everyone else to be valuable. We're here, now, moving through our own lives, shaped by our experiences, our struggles, and our happiness, just like a snowflake shaped by the wind, warmth, and height.

And Then, There's the Impact We Make

When a snowflake lands, it melts, yes, but it also adds something. It becomes part of something bigger: a snowdrift, a glacier, a warm blanket for seeds to grow. In the same way, our individuality doesn't exist alone. Our differences help communities grow, spark change, and inspire others to shine.

Think of the artist who painted outside the rules. The teacher who stayed late to help. The quiet neighbor who brought food when you needed it. The friend who laughed at your funny jokes. Each of us leaves little ripples, sometimes not even noticed, that change the world in small, important ways. Like snowflakes, we don't have to be huge to be important.

[2] E.E. Cummings once said, "To be no-body-but-yourself, in a world which is doing its

---

2. The quote is from a 1955 address published in a collection of his work. In the address, Cummings offered advice to young people who wanted to be poets (which he defined in a broad sense as being a "real" or authentic person).

best, night and day, to make you everybody else, means to fight the hardest battle which any human being can fight." This battle isn't loud or flashy; it's fought in small moments, choosing authenticity over approval, curiosity over conformity, vulnerability over performance.

It's in deciding to wear the bright scarf when everyone else wears gray. It's in saying, "I see it differently," when silence would be easier. It's in nurturing the dream that doesn't fit neatly into a PowerPoint slide. It's in letting your snowflake fall exactly as it is meant to.

And perhaps that's why winter, for all its cold, feels so deeply comforting. It doesn't demand productivity. It doesn't measure success in output. It simply invites us to witness beauty in stillness and variety. It reminds us that we don't have to earn our place in the world. We are already part of the pattern, necessary, irreplaceable, and stunning in our specificity.

So, the next time you're tempted to shrink yourself, afraid your thoughts are too strange, your emotions too intense, your dreams too big, step outside. Watch the snow fall. Catch a flake if you can (a dark cloth helps, breathe gently, don't rush). Marvel at its complexity. Then remember you, too, are a masterpiece in motion.

Not that you're perfect, but that you are real. Your path has been shaped by forces no one else has faced. Your light, your voice, your presence, however brief, add dimension to the world that nothing else could.

We aren't meant to be copies. We aren't meant to be mass-produced. We are meant to spiral down through life, each on our own quiet trajectory, leaving behind something that only we could have offered.

So be as distinct as a snowflake.

Twirl in your uniqueness.

Lessons from a Frozen Pond

As winter wraps us in its icy hug and the days get shorter and more fragile, nature changes gently. The world seems to slow down a bit. Leaves, once so bright and full of life, are now covered in a snowy blanket. The wind feels a bit sharper. Plus, the water, which always flows, changes too. Ponds and puddles, once full from rain and morning dew, turn into smooth, shiny surfaces. Some are like perfect mirrors of the sky, while others ripple and buckle, like water dancing when the cold suddenly stopped, mid-breath, when it finally stopped.

Icicles grow along the eaves and branches, like crystal spears made from the melting and freezing of water, sparkling like nature's chandeliers. They catch the pale winter light and bend it into something almost magical, delicate, dangerous, and beautiful all at once. But there's more to this than just science. Freezing, the change from liquid to solid, from flowing to forming, is not just a scientific thing. It's a symbol. It's a quiet lesson in how we can be strong.

Water doesn't fight the cold. It doesn't complain about the drop in temperature. It just changes. It hardens, not because it gives up, but because it protects itself. And even though the ice looks solid, life is still there.

Fish swim slowly, their bodies working less, their movements careful and dreamy. Frogs hide in the mud, their hearts beating only a few times a minute. Insects and larvae hang in time, waiting. There's no sadness in this stillness, just trust. Trust that the ice will stay strong. Trust that the seasons will change. Trust that warmth will come back.

The pond, even though it looks so still, isn't dead. It's just resting.

There's a kind of beauty in this, how stillness can hide movement, how silence can be filled with possibilities. Not every season is for doing things. Not every day needs to be busy.

Sometimes, the bravest thing we can do is to stop and take a breath.

To let ourselves freeze over, not out of despair, but out of strength. To hold our shape, even when the world feels harsh and unyielding.

I remember this truth most vividly not from a science book, but from a frozen pond near my childhood home.

When I was a young teenager, winter wasn't just a season; it was an invitation. Every December, if the cold held long enough, the ponds between our neighborhood homes would freeze several inches thick. We measured the thickness of the ice to make sure it would hold us without breaking through. Sometimes pushing the boundaries of safety, but the ice was calling. We would rush outside with skates tied to our backs, sticks in hand, gloves stuffed with plastic bags to keep our fingers from going numb.

There was no rink. No scoreboard. No fancy gear. Just ice, a puck, and the boundless energy of youth.

We'd clear the snow with hockey sticks and shovels, carving out a rough rectangle in the middle of the ice. The snowbanks and slope of the land were enough to keep the puck from sliding away too far. We'd play until our toes tingled, then huddle around a makeshift fire built from wood stored for use during our skating adventures.

That fire, its crackle, its warmth, the way it turned frozen mittens into damp rags, was as much a part of the ritual as the game itself. At times, we would roast marshmallows over the flames, watching them catch fire before pulling them back to puff into golden, gooey perfection. We'd sandwich them between graham crackers and chocolate, laughing as our fingers fumbled with the sticky mess.

These were not gourmet s'mores. They were survival snacks. But they tasted like joy.

And as we warmed ourselves, we'd talk; about school, any silly topic that came to mind, and about dreams that felt both impossibly far and just within reach. The cold wrapped around us, the fire pulled us inward, and for a few golden hours, everything felt simple.

Even now, decades later, that fire still brings a smile to my face. I remember it when I'm with friends around winter bonfires, watching kids skate on frozen lakes, or savoring the sweet, charred taste of a perfectly toasted marshmallow. It's in the quiet moments, like watching steam rise from a cup of hot chocolate, or the unspoken understanding that sometimes, all you need is to be together.

Skating on that thin, black ice was pure magic. There was a kind of poetry in the glide, how your body leaned into the flow, how the scrape of steel against ice became a rhythm, a song. And hockey, the passing, the checking, the sudden sprint toward the goal, wasn't just a game. It was a dance of coordination, instinct, and trust. You learned to read your teammates' moves without even saying a word. You knew when to charge forward and when to hold back. You discovered that even on the coldest day, your heart could burn with such intensity.

As I watch our grandson glide across the sparkling, climate-controlled ice rink, dressed in cutting-edge gear, holding a top-of-the-line composite stick, his custom skates carving perfect arcs, I can't help but smile. The arena buzzes with modern precision: flawless ice, advanced safety gear, and coaches using tablets to analyze every move. Yet, my thoughts drift back to my own winters, spent on nature's rink, the frozen ponds that stretched like bumpy ice beneath gray winter skies. There were no Zambonis, only brooms and hope. Our skates were passed down, worn thin, laced tightly over wool socks. Wooden sticks were splintered with use, taped at the blade and shaft, yet cherished like treasures. The cold nipped at our cheeks, the ice cracked beneath us, and the wind carried laughter through the bare trees. We played not for scouts or scholarships, but for the sheer joy of movement, of friendship, of a puck sent flying toward a mittened goalie. There was simplicity in those days, an innocence born of raw elements and unstructured play. And though I marvel at today's advancements, I also recognize the enduring spirit of the game. It's not in the gear or the rinks, but in the heartbeat of winter, the thrill of a forward stride, the bond between players. What's changed is the world around the game, but the soul of it, the love of skating under open skies or bright lights, remains beautifully unchanged. That legacy, passed from frozen pond to polished ice, is the true gift I carry, and now, proudly, pass on.

Winter, in its stillness, is not idle rest. That pause is not failure. That sometimes, the most powerful thing you can do is to be still, to let yourself solidify, to become a surface strong enough to hold others. Like the water, we too are asked to change form. There are times when life demands fluidity, when we must adapt, flow, respond. But there are also times when we must harden. When we must set boundaries. When we must say no. When we must endure.

Resilience isn't just about getting back up after a fall. It's about staying strong when things get tough. It's about making something so solid that others can glide over it without breaking it. It's about providing stability while still having a vibrant world underneath.

The ice shows us this. So do winters. And maybe, in our fast-paced, connected, always-on world, we need these seasonal reminders more than ever. We rush from one thing to another. We scroll through endless information. We think being busy means we're doing something important. The pond doesn't freeze because it's idle; it freezes because it's perfectly in tune with its environment. Just like the pond, we're all part of a natural cycle, constantly changing and adapting.

The pond reminded us that even when things are tough, there's still room to have fun, try new things, and chase happiness.

Chapter Nine

The Season of Heartfelt Sorrow

Even the most beautiful mountains and peaceful rivers experience their own seasons of sadness; heavy rains flood valleys, fierce hurricanes tear at coastlines, and volcanoes erupt with a roar of loss. These natural disasters remind us that grief is a natural part of life, a constant rhythm that flows through both the earth and our hearts. Just as the forest grows new shoots after a fire and the ocean calms after a storm, we too go through cycles of mourning, whether for a dear friend, a cherished dream, or the passage of time. By understanding that our personal struggles are like the planet's story, we find comfort in the idea that every tear-filled night is followed by a new day. Let this shared dance of loss and renewal encourage us to honor our grief, nurture the seeds of hope it creates, and move forward with the quiet confidence that, like nature, we are strong enough to bloom again.

Grandparents and Parents leave this Earth

The fall of 1975 was a season that left a lasting mark on my childhood. I saw the unstoppable passage of time in my grandmother and grandfather's frail, trembling hands, each reaching toward the inevitable end of life. I was fifteen then, on the brink of becoming invincible and starting to understand that life, like the ever-changing seasons, is a cycle of birth, growth, decline, and renewal.

My grandmother, whom I loved dearly as Mabel, was a constant reminder of love and compassion. We lived in the same house as our grandparents until I was twelve, and I have so many cherished memories of my early childhood with them. At seventy-four, my grandmother was a wiry woman with silver hair tied neatly, eyes that sparkled like polished amber, and a laugh that could bring a smile to even the grumpiest of relatives. Her kitchen was a haven of scents, freshly baked bread, simmering beans, and the delicious aroma of apple pie that seemed to rise with the sun each morning. In September of that year, the air started to cool; cancer had tightened its deadly hold.

On the day my grandmother passed away, I remember the sky was a soft gray, and there was a deep quiet that made the world feel reverent. I stood at the entrance of the small church, feeling an inexplicable emptiness in my chest, a void that went beyond just missing my grandmother and showed me for the first time that even the most vibrant things must eventually fade away. The funeral was simple: family and friends gathered. I looked at my grandmother's closed eyes and saw for the first time how her eyelids seemed to hold a story, a lifetime of whispered advice, lullabies, and whispered prayers. In that moment, death became real, a doorway that had opened for her, and through which I saw the continuity of life itself.

Me looking at my grand-ma holding my older brother

I remember, as a child, discovering my grandmother's old coloring book, thin and worn. The cover was faded, like a ghost of its original colors, tucked away in a secretariat. The pages, yellowed and fragile, seemed to tell stories of her childhood. I traced the outline of a train track on one page, where the lines seemed to meet at a single point on the horizon, as if they were going on forever. When I showed it to my grandmother, I asked, "What makes these lines so special?" She smiled, her eyes crinkling with memories, and said, "They showed us how to see things differently."

The coloring book was from the early 1900s. Inside the cover page, she wrote, " Mabel Christmas 1911," a time when art was a quiet way to stand out from the everyday. My grandmother had filled some of its pages with crayons and dreams, learning to make flat paper look deep. The train track drawing, a simple exercise in perspective, became our starting point. She explained how two straight tracks, even though they were technically parallel, had to meet to trick the eye into thinking they were stretching "forever." "Start by drawing the rails close together," she told me, "but then widen the space as they get closer to the bottom of the page. The trick is to make the paper look so beautiful that it feels real."

My grandmother's coloring book

As she spoke, I was amazed by how a child's simple coloring tool had evolved into a profound lesson in perception. I realized that perspective wasn't just a technique; it was a way of thinking. My grandmother, who had endured wars, lost parents, and likely walked miles to school, had carried this lesson beyond art. "Life's like that track," she said, her voice steady. "You can't see the end of it, but you keep drawing the rails anyway. And if you aim them right, they'll take you somewhere."

That afternoon, we spent what seemed like hours examining her old drawings. A small crayon landscape turned into a meditation on scale: a tiny house shrinking as it neared the distant hills, a tree's branches tapering to suggest wind sweeping across the page. My grandmother's wrinkled hands once held the same crayons as a child with clumsy urgency. "They said coloring was just a hobby," she mused, "but it taught me how to think. How to see the distance between where I was and where I wanted to be."

Her words stayed with me long after she tucked the book back into the secretariat. I thought about the train tracks, how their lines, though diverging, became a promise of convergence. Isn't that what we all seek? A way to bridge the gap between our present and our dreams, our struggles, and our purpose? Perspective isn't just about seeing the horizon—it's about believing the path exists to reach it.

Years later, when I stand before a blank canvas or a challenging crossroads, I return to my grandmother's lesson. The world feels flatter now, fractured by noise and immediacy, but the principle holds: to create depth, we must first embrace the vanishing point. We must draw our own rails, even when the horizon is uncertain. My grandmother's train tracks are etched into my mind, a reminder that perspective is a choice. A decision to step back, to reframe, to find the lines that make the impossible feel nearby.

The coloring book now sits on my shelf, its delicate pages a reminder of how small things can leave a lasting impact on our lives. My grandmother passed away, but her voice lives on, resonating in every line and distant horizon I dare to dream of. She taught me that art and life aren't about the tools we have, but how we use them to see. To color beyond the page's boundaries and to believe, with each stroke, that the path will guide us forward.

So, when the world feels too small, I think of her train tracks. I think of the child who learned to make paper lie so beautifully that it became real. And I remember: the horizon isn't an end. It's an invitation.

Just two months later, in November, the cold of winter once again crept into our home and into my very bones. The world outside was a collection of frosted leaves and early snow, while inside, a different kind of cold lingered, an emotional frost that settled on the hearth where my grandfather, whom I called Ervin, who would sit by the coal furnace in the basement keeping watch over the furnace fire, spinning tales of his youth and the love that had blossomed between him and Mabel. At seventy-five, Ervin's once-steady voice now carried a sorrowful note with the passing of Mabel, his lifelong companion. Ervin suffered a heart attack and passed away on that bitter November afternoon.

The second funeral felt like a reflection of the first, but it was heavier. My father, already wrestling with grief, seemed to drift, his eyes filled with tears that wouldn't come. He, usually so calm, leaned against the kitchen counter, his arms shaking as he tried to hold back a sob that threatened to break through his usual composure. I stood there, feeling the weight of the world on my shoulders, and for the first time, I understood that grief isn't just a single moment but a river that flows through our lives, carving new paths and changing our hearts.

As winter came and the first snowflakes fell, I started to notice patterns; cycle, like the seasons, that connected birth, death, and rebirth. The snow, cold and still, also held the promise of spring. It reminded me that just as the earth needs to be covered in frost before new shoots can grow, we, too, need to experience loss to truly appreciate growth. My grandparents' passing made me realize how fragile life is, but it also showed me the strength in the human spirit. Their lives, though over, left behind seeds of values, stories, and love that would grow in the generations to come.

I recall sitting at the kitchen table one evening, the old oak chair creaking beneath me, and listening to the soft hum of the refrigerator as my mother poured hot chocolate into two mismatched cups. The steam curled like the lingering tendrils of my grandparents' presence, warm and fleeting. She told me about the quiet mornings she'd spent with my grandmother, how they'd knead dough together in the cool of dawn, flour dusting the counter like early snow, or how my grandmother would hum old songs while doing her laundry. She spoke of laughter over burnt pies, cinnamon-roll recipes, or other foods that she liked to prepare. Her mother-in-law had a way of making her feel like one of the family. Those stories wrapped around me like the warmth of the mug in my hands, and for the first time, I understood that grief wasn't just absence—it was also presence in another form. The words settled deep within me, intertwining with my own budding understanding that death is not an abrupt end but a transition, a return to the earth that nourishes, a return to the collective memory that sustains.

The months turned to years, and the pain of that 1975 winter gradually softened, like the edge of a stone smoothed by the constant flow of a river. I grew older, took on responsibilities, and, like the sprouting seedlings in spring, I began to sprout my own branches, reaching toward the sky while staying rooted in the fertile soil left by my grandparents. Their lessons, Mabel's patience, Grandpa's stories, their unyielding love for family became compass points guiding me through my own trials: the loss of friends, the uncertainties of adulthood, and the inevitable confrontations with my own mortality as I aged. Each time I felt the cold grip of doubt, I would recall that crisp November night, the sound of wind rustling through bare trees, and realize that just as those trees shed their leaves only to bloom again, I too could let go of old fears and welcome new growth.

In hindsight, the twin losses of 1975 were not merely tragedies but pivotal milestones that carved a deeper awareness of life's cyclical nature into my soul. They taught me that grief, while painful, is also a testament to love, an affirmation that we have truly lived. Decades later, as I stood at the edge of my own journey through profound loss, I began to understand the truth in those words. The seasons of my life shifted irrevocably when my parents passed away, each departure etching into my being the wisdom of acceptance, love, and the sacred interplay of endings and new beginnings.

My mother's journey with Alzheimer's was a slow, gentle unraveling, a quiet watch as the person I loved slowly faded into shadows, leaving only pieces of who she once was. For years, I watched her mind slowly crumble, the vibrant woman who had taught me to find joy in the everyday now lost in a world where even her own children felt like strangers. Her illness wasn't just one big storm but a constant tide, slowly wearing away the shore of her identity until only a faint echo remained. When she finally passed away on November 27, 2014, at the age of 79, there was a strange quiet in the room, as if life itself had paused to honor her. Even though her body was frail, her presence felt more monumental than ever.

As her final breath left her, my mind didn't focus on the pain of loss but instead drifted to warm memories, a memory of her in the kitchen, sleeves rolled up, coaxing life into a dough of flour and butter, cinnamon swirling like gold dust on the counter. She was making rolls, not just for show; they were meant to comfort a child's loneliness after a long day at school. She'd pull a pan of just-baked rolls from the oven, or reheat a pan of rolls she prepared earlier, pair them with a cup of rich hot chocolate, and set it before me as if it were a feast. "Nourishment for the soul," she'd say, her eyes crinkling. Even now, when illness or weariness drags me down, I crave hot chocolate and cinnamon rolls.

Years earlier, she had asked me to sing the song "Sheltered in the Arms of God" at her funeral, a request I fulfilled with trembling hands and a heart so heavy it felt like it anchored me to the earth. But in that moment, I felt her love wrap around me like a spiritual embrace, a reminder that even in absence, she would always be a part of me.

Her care touched me in ways beyond the kitchen. I remember her on a bright afternoon, mending my pants with such skill that it felt as if she were mending a broken heart. She rarely bought me new clothes, preferring to fix the old with patience and a little lace or button. She'd say, "Imperfect things are still beautiful," her voice like a soothing lullaby. (It could also be that we didn't have much money to buy new clothing) Those patched pants became my armor, a reminder of her belief that I could handle anything. Even when I was most vulnerable, she taught me to find strength in repair, turning imperfection into a story.

And how could I forget the nights she read to me, her voice my only guide through the storms of my childhood fears? She'd snuggle beside me on the couch, holding the worn pages of Bible stories or Charlotte's Web or other books, her voice soft but steady. Her stories were more than words; they were doors to courage, a quiet belief that love could overcome any challenge. Even when I was too old to admit how much I needed it, her voice stayed with me, a whisper of wisdom to turn to when life's twists became too dark.

Watching her pass didn't take away these truths. It made them even more real. In her final days, her body was different, her voice reduced to soft breaths. But her spirit remained the same. When I share those stories of rolls with others, whether it's a friend dealing with grief, a neighbor facing a cold morning, or a stranger with tears in their eyes, I'm not just sharing stories of food. I'm passing on her legacy: the idea that love isn't just an idea. It's the warmth of a kitchen, the patience of a needle, the magic of a story whispered in the dark. It's the stubborn light that shines even after death.

In many ways, my mother's passing wasn't really an end, but more like baking, the layers of her lessons rising and solidifying into something that will last forever. I don't need her physically present to feel her. She lives on in the cinnamon I sprinkle with care, in the way I fix things. I know how powerful a stitch can be. Her love became a strength I carry, a recipe I'll never let fade. Today, as I enjoy fresh rolls from the oven, their scent mingling with the echoes of her laughter, I realize that grief can be comforting, too. When I remember how deeply she loved, I'm reminded of how deeply I'm still loved. And that, I think, was her greatest gift: to teach me that love endures even beyond the walls of the room where we say goodbye.

Grief doesn't always follow a straight path. Six years later, I faced another goodbye when my father, who grieved in the shadow of my mother's loss, passed away on February 20, 2020, at age 89 after a sudden heart attack. His death was sudden, a final act that didn't follow the slow, sacred rhythm of grief's preparation. Yet I found echoes of my mother's journey in the stories he left behind, the music, the laughter, the way he had woven his life into the fabric of our family's history.

When my sister quietly told me my father had passed away, a deep silence settled over the usual morning chaos. I was suddenly back in a sun-dappled afternoon when I was six, and my father had shown me how to draw a horse. He often drew horses and told stories about his childhood, riding a retired racehorse without a saddle. When I was seven, my mother gave me a paint-by-number set of watercolors with a horse on it. Now, as I sit quietly at home, the memory of that first horse, bright, a little rough, but completely mine, is still so vivid. It reminds me that every line (maybe not every line) he drew in my life still guides me, and that the love he put into a simple drawing is like the steady marks I'll use to paint the rest of my days: brave, kind, and always moving forward.

My paint-by-numbers horse painting

My father often talked about the cast-iron penny bank that had been his constant toy since he was a kid. He'd tell stories about how its deep, mottled surface, with the faint outline of a grinning pig, felt so cool and solid in his hand, and how heavy it made him feel, like it held all sorts of possibilities. He spent many hours playing with the penny bank on the floor, letting his imagination run free. He saved every penny he could, putting them into the slot with a satisfying clink that made him feel like he was winning something small in his room. The bank wasn't just for money; it was a symbol of patience and discipline, like a game where he imagined building a kingdom from just a few cents. Years later, the memory was still clear, a reminder of a time when being happy could come from the little things, and the future seemed as big as the pennies that kept falling into that unyielding iron pig.

My dad's penny bank

When I was in my teens, my dad continued his musical adventures by forming a family quartet with me and my two older brothers. At his funeral, my brother and I sang one of my dad's favorite quartet songs. We sang along to a recording that included both his part and our late brother's, who had passed away before him, as if for one last time. In that song, I felt their presence, forever connected in time but still so real in my heart. That moment showed me how life is always turning, not just moving forward, but like a dance where endings lead us to really understand things.

These losses became mirrors, reflecting the profound interconnectedness of love and loss. My mother's illness taught me patience and the quiet strength of being present when words fail. My father's final breath reminded me to cherish the fleeting moments of connection, for life hangs by the thinnest threads. Together, they wove a web of understanding: that grief is not a failure but a measure of how deeply we have loved. Each tear shed, each memory treasured, becomes a seed planted in the fertile soil of the soul.

There is a sacred rhythm to these journeys of letting go. Nature itself offers a metaphor: the falling leaves that nourish the earth, the storms that cleanse the air, the winter that makes way for spring. My parents' deaths did not erase the joy of their lives but magnified it. I began to see that their absence was not a void but a continuation, a presence reshaped by love's resilience. My mother's dementia may have stolen her memory, but never her legacy. My father's sudden departure may have left no warning, but his laughter and songs endure in the stories we share. Like the old oak tree that grows around the fence post, life finds a way to adapt, to bend without breaking.

Over the years since my parents passed away, I've come to see my grief as a kind of spiritual journey. It's taught me to listen to my heart, to sit in the quiet of sorrow without fear, and to understand that love doesn't fade with death but transforms. The rituals of mourning, the songs, the memories, the shared tears, became windows to this truth. When I sang for my mother, I didn't say goodbye but "until we meet again." When I sang with my brother and my father's and my late brother's voices on the recording, I felt the joy of reunion in the moment. Grief, I've learned, is a living bridge between what was and what will be.

Now, as I walk through the days that follow these milestones, I carry their lessons like lanterns in the dark. I've learned that life's cycles are not to be feared but honored. The loss of my parents didn't erase my joy in living but deepened my reverence for every sunrise, every shared meal, every hand that was held.

They have become silent guides, reminding me that the meaning of a life well-lived lies not in avoiding pain but in allowing it to shape us into more compassionate and resilient vessels.

Perhaps the greatest gift of these losses is the way they have softened my edges, teaching me that grief is not the opposite of joy but its shadow. To love fully is to grieve fully, and in that paradox lies the essence of being human. My parents' deaths didn't end their story; they became part of a larger narrative, one where love outlives death, where the cycle of life continues not in a circle but in an ever-expanding spiral, carrying us toward a deeper understanding of what it means to be alive.

In the end, the twin losses of my parents were not tragedies but sacred transitions, gateways to wisdom. They showed me that the soul is not bound by time, that love leaves footprints on our hearts, and that grief, when embraced, becomes a teacher. As I walk forward, I do so not in mourning but in gratitude, knowing that in loss, there is life; in sorrow, there is beauty; and in the echoes of their voices, there is an unbroken thread connecting all of us to the eternal dance of existence.

Seeing the Sacred in the Small

Finding God's Glory in Nature's Quiet Wisdom

In a world that's always rushing and chasing after the big, flashy things, we sometimes overlook the deep wisdom hidden in the simplest parts of nature. Think about the gentle rustle of leaves in the fall, the way a fern unfurls in the spring, or how dawn paints the sky with colors so delicate they're almost too beautiful to describe. These aren't just random events; they're special invitations, like whispers from the heart of God, encouraging us to appreciate not only the amazing miracles He creates but also the tiny, fragile, and fleeting moments. God's creativity isn't just found in the loud, dramatic moments; it's also in the everyday, the things we might not notice. It's not just in the thunder, but in the flutter of a moth's wing and the patience of a seed growing into a tree.

The Quiet Magnificence of Creation

Think of creation as a beautiful symphony, full of tiny, detailed notes. Take a snowflake, for example: each one is a unique six-sided crystal of ice, a masterpiece made by the careful balance of temperature, humidity, and time. Even though they're all different, no two snowflakes are the same, but they all follow a fascinating mathematical pattern. The honeybee's dance is another example. It tells the bee colony where to find food with amazing accuracy, a language so complex that scientists were amazed for ages. Even a simple stalk of corn, growing strong and tall from the ground, shows a quiet strength. Its green tassels sway in the wind, like a gentle song of growth, while its roots soak up nutrients from the earth, creating a beautiful web of life hidden beneath the surface.

The Fibonacci sequence, a series of numbers in which each number is the sum of the two before it, appears in the spiral of a seashell or the way petals are arranged on a sunflower, showing a divine order in the natural world. The way a dragonfly's wings shimmer, made of tiny structures that play with light, is a true engineering wonder. Even lichen, a team of fungi and algae living together on rocks, shows beautiful teamwork that's hard for us to understand. When we take the time to look closely at these details, we start to see not just individual parts, but how everything in nature fits together perfectly.

The Crisis of Missing the Obvious

In today's fast-paced world, it's easy to miss the little things. We're always chasing big wins and amazing moments. The media loves to make a fuss, and we celebrate the loudest voices. So, we often focus on the "big fireworks," like answered prayers, dramatic changes, or life-changing insights. While these are powerful, they can sometimes become our only way to see God's presence, and we might miss the quiet ways He speaks to us. But how can we see the extraordinary if we've never learned to notice the ordinary?

When we're busy solving problems, meeting deadlines, or trying to reach our goals, we might end up like the man who walks past a garden but never stops to admire the roses. The natural rhythm of life, the changing seasons, the patience needed for a flower to bloom aren't just a backdrop to our stories.

Looking at the small details is like having a special job. The farmer who plants seeds, the caregiver who bandages wounds, the artist who mixes colors to paint a sunset, all these people are part of the divine rhythm of creation and healing. Even the everyday tasks, like fixing clothes, taking care of kids, or tending to a garden, become special when we see their purpose.

Think about a nautilus shell spiraling or a supernova exploding. They both show the same kind of mathematical beauty. A spider's web is like a reflection of divine order, just like a galaxy dances.

The beauty of these details isn't in how big they are, but in how they fit together with everything else. They're like tiny notes in the big story of faith, and looking at them helps us understand the mysteries of eternity.

A Call to Slow Down and See

So, what's our move? To live with reverence, we need to slow down. Imagine strolling through a park, not just for exercise, but to really listen to the trees. Or maybe sitting with a cup of coffee, not just to get a caffeine boost, but to watch the steam rise like the breath of creation. And when you gaze at the stars, remember that the light reaching your eyes might have been traveling for centuries.

This isn't just about escaping; it's about actively choosing to see the world as it truly is. It takes some discipline to tune out the noise and focus on what truly matters. It also means being humble enough to realize that we don't control life's rhythm, only participate in it.

Next time you see a snowflake landing on a leaf, a bee buzzing around a flower, or a stalk of corn reaching for the sun, remember these aren't distractions from faith, but invitations into it. Paying attention to them is like hearing His voice anew, seeing with the eyes of faith, speaking with the tongue of wonder, and living with the heart of a child who has never stopped being amazed.

In the end, the quiet wisdom of the world is worth heeding. It's a reflection of the divine. And by noticing its smallest wonders, we find that the God of the cosmos is also the God of the everyday, a God who meets us, not just in the thunder, but in the quiet moments.

The Invitation to See

We're living in a world where we're constantly distracted. Screens are always buzzing with urgent messages, our minds are racing from one thing to the next, and we're always listening to the digital noise of notifications, each one promising something important. We're taking in so much information in a day that our ancestors never saw in their whole lives, but how much of it do we really take in? In our never-ending search for the new, for efficiency, and seeing amazing things, we've forgotten how to really see. We just glance, scroll, and move on, never stopping long enough to really see something and understand its hidden beauty. And in all this rushing, we miss the special things that are right there, whispering in the quiet moments between all the noise and hurry.

But what if we decided to slow down?

Imagine stepping away from everything, leaving the world behind, and kneeling to look at a single wildflower swaying in the wind. Not to take a picture or just think about it for a moment, but to really see it, the tiny veins in its petals, how it bends without breaking, and the little bug crawling along its stem like a tiny pilgrim on a sacred journey. Or picture yourself standing by a stream, not just passing by, but stopping to listen, not just hearing the water, but really listening to its song as it dances over old stones, carving stories into the earth with patient persistence. Something changes in those moments. Your breathing slows down. Your mind quiets. You start to see a harmony beneath the surface, a quiet order, a gentle pulse that suggests this world isn't random, but it's loved. This isn't just feeling sentimental. This is a spiritual awakening, the soul remembering its first language: wonder, reverence, and worship.

Imagine a snowflake, a beautiful, quiet creation that falls with a gentle purpose. Scientists are amazed by its perfect shape, and poets see it as a frozen star. Who makes something so detailed that it might melt before we even see it? Who finds joy in designing something so amazing that no one will ever see it? Creating is its own kind of happiness.

This is the hidden music of creation, a huge, connected web of life where everything is linked. The ant carries its load not for fame, but to help the colony live. The bee, though it only lives a short time, visits lots of flowers, helping them grow in service to something much bigger than itself. The stream, patient and steady, carves canyons over many years. The cornstalk grows slowly, showing us how faithful the seasons are.

These aren't just random things happening in nature. They're pieces in a special, carefully made picture. And when we really look at them, not just look, but really see, we start to hear the music. We hear it in how things connect: the bird that eats the insect that eats the leaf that drinks the sunlight; the river that flows into the ocean that feeds the clouds that bring rain to the field. Creation isn't a mess; it's a connection. Everything depends on something else. Every life helps something else.

Have you ever really watched a bee at work? Not just seeing it, but truly witnessing it, the way it dives into a flower, its fuzzy legs covered in golden pollen, its wings flapping in a blur of devotion? In that moment, you're not just watching nature; you're witnessing ministry. The bee doesn't know it, but it's doing something bigger than itself, supporting life, nourishing ecosystems, reminding us that no job is too small. Isn't that like looking at our own lives? We might feel insignificant, like just one voice in a crowd, one prayer lost in the wind, one act of kindness ignored.

We've all heard the saying: "You can't see the forest for the trees." But what if it's the other way around? What if the best way to really understand the forest, the huge, amazing picture of God's plan, is to first love the trees? When we take time to look at a single leaf, its shape, its color, how it turns toward the light, we start to see how everything is connected, how everything depends on each other. We begin to understand not just what's happening, but why.

Creation isn't just pretty scenery. It's a message. It speaks. It tells us things. But we must be quiet enough to hear. We must calm down inside to hear what's outside. When we focus on the little things, we start to see the big picture. A dandelion growing through concrete is like a story about strength. A starry sky is like a place of wonder.

Chapter Eleven

The Call to Care

Embracing the Small, Living the Great

There's a gentle, almost surprising truth at the heart of a truly happy life: the more we cherish the little things in creation, the more we feel we need to take care of them. When we see the world not just as stuff to use but as a sacred gift from the Creator, we naturally want to protect it. We start tending to the earth, watching over the tiny pollinators that buzz from flower to flower, planting trees that will outlive us, and saving water that sustains us all. In this simple act of caring, our love for creation flows through us, shaping how we think, what we do, and ultimately, where we're headed.

A Practice of Presence

So, how do we start this journey of respectful care? It begins with being present, really noticing the world around us without rushing. Today, step outside. Find a tree that catches your eye. Sit under its shade and let the sunlight play on your skin. Watch a bird land on a branch; follow an ant as it carries its load, walking with purpose across the ground. Lie on the grass and feel the earth beneath you, letting the clouds drift by in their slow, beautiful dance. Breathe. Listen. Receive.

Don't jump to conclusions or turn the scene into a sermon before it's even settled. Let the experience just be, let it happen. Let the rustling leaves, the gentle buzzing of wings, the distant sound of a stream become the way God speaks to us. In that quiet, we realize that the Master Plan isn't something we can just think about; it's something we feel with our hearts. It's not just in the big things in the universe, but also in the small, beautiful moments like a bee coming back to its hive, a stream flowing over rocks, or a single leaf turning toward the sun. In these tiny miracles, we see the great love that holds everything together, and that love brings us closer to where we truly belong.

Finding Stillness on the Edge of the Lake

Weekends have a special, almost magical rhythm that the world sometimes overlooks. My wife and I escape the hustle and bustle, lace up our shoes, and wander along the winding forest paths that hug the lake's edge. The path is well known, but each step feels like a fresh adventure, with every wildflower waving its bright colors, every ancient oak standing as a silent witness to time.

The forest is like a living museum. We stop by a patch of lupines, their purple trumpets swaying in the soft breeze, and breathe in the fresh scent of pine and damp earth. A maple tree, twisted by years of wind, stretches its branches wide like a storyteller's arms, reminding us that beauty often comes in its own unique way. In these moments, our focus is on the feel of a leaf, the buzzing of insects, and the gentle rustle of a squirrel scurrying for cover. It's a gentle reminder that the big stories we chase, like career achievements or endless to-do lists, are all built on these small, perfect moments.

As we leave the shade, we reach the lake's smooth surface. The water's small ripples invite the sky to spill into it. Across the gentle ripples, people in canoes glide by, their paddles slicing the silence with soft sighs. A family in a paddleboat laughs, their joy spreading out, and for a moment, we share their happiness without saying a word. It's a simple connection: strangers, nature, and the unspoken understanding that today is a gift.

We find a bench by the water and share a small snack: fresh berries, a slice of cheese, a crumb of crusty bread, or a granola bar. We eat slowly, enjoying not just the taste but the pause itself. The lake listens as we talk about everything and nothing, about our future, old jokes, and the quiet hope that we might stay a little longer in this peaceful corner of time. The world around us keeps its gentle dance going: a dragonfly zips by, a leaf drifts, and the wind whispers through the reeds.

When we finally rise, the forest seems to exhale with us, as if it, too, recognizes the fleeting nature of our visit. We walk back to our car with a lighter step, carrying the lake's stillness in our pockets, a reminder that life's most profound moments are often the unplanned, unhurried ones.

Tomorrow is never promised. The next sunrise might find us in a different place, or perhaps the same trail, but the truth remains: if we don't make space to pause, to breathe, to truly see the world around us, we risk missing the very things that make life worth living. So, wherever you are, find your lake, be it literal or metaphorical, sit down, enjoy a simple snack, and let the world's whisper remind you that every breath is a chance to be present, to love, and to appreciate the incredible mosaic of life that unfolds, one leaf, one ripple, one shared smile at a time.

"I'm Next in Line": A Personal Encounter with the Master Plan

I didn't quite grasp this paradox of being small yet great until I was standing in the quiet after a loss. Years after my grandfather passed, my father, who usually kept his words to himself (though he did enjoy chatting), sat me down and said, "Now I'm next in line." I was in my twenties, and his words didn't hit me with sorrow, but with a surprising sense of comfort. It felt like a bridge had been built between me and what was to come, a cushion that softened the edge of death. My father's quiet presence was a shield, not from the reality of mortality, but from how soon it would be. He was like a link in a chain that stretched back through generations and into the future.

Time, as it always does, kept moving forward. I watched his hair turn gray, his hands get a little shaky, and his steps slow down on the paths we routinely walked together. Then, one day, he was gone. The shield disappeared, and I was standing alone at the edge of my own later years. The words "next in line" now had a different meaning. They weren't a promise of protection anymore; they were a reminder of what I had to do, a call to carry on the trust that had been placed in me.

I remember the day we took a photo with four generations, my dad, me, my son, and my grandson, sitting around a table eating lunch.

Four generations

Dad was the oldest, his silver hair catching the afternoon light that streamed through the curtains. He wore his favorite shirt and suspenders, a reminder that he still tended the garden (though Mom did most of the work). My son sat beside him, my grandson in front, the bridge between his time and mine, feeling the weight of the stories he had passed down to me: tales of riding a horse without a saddle, of helping his grandfather build a bookshelf, of a life built with steady, unhurried hands. I was at the end, like a bookend, marking the end of the generations.

The camera clicked, and for a moment, everything seemed to disappear. In that instant, we weren't just a family photo; we were a snapshot of our lives. My dad's eyes sparkled with a quiet pride, knowing his story would live on beyond the flash. My son's smile made it clear he was determined to keep that flame burning for his own child. And my grandson, still too young to grasp it, was already the brightest light, his innocence like fresh wood ready to catch fire.

Several years before my father passed away, he and I were sitting at the kitchen table, the faint smell of coffee filling the air. Before us were small pieces of old silo board, its surface marked with the gentle lines of a life well-lived. My father, who wasn't one for big gestures, had picked this simple material for a gift that was far more precious than any wrapped present: a piece of himself, carved into Christmas keepsakes for each of his children. The lines on his face deepened, just like the grooves in the wood. Part of an old silo on the farm. It had fallen apart years ago, but it was strong; it had held up a lifetime of harvests.

Dad signing the old silo boards

In that moment, I didn't quite understand the depth of what he was saying. He wasn't just signing wood; he was carving out a legacy. Each signature was a promise that his story would live on through ours. The silo board, once a silent guardian of work and food, became a vessel for love.

Years later, after the silo had completely fallen apart and the farm had been taken over by someone new, I found myself holding my father's wooden token in the quiet after his passing. Its edges had softened with time, but the letters he'd written were still clear and sharp, as if they were fighting against decay. I remembered that kitchen scene, how he paused before writing his name, his brow furrowed not with effort, but with purpose.

Signed pieces of silo board

In his quiet wisdom, he had created something that would last beyond him, something that spoke of perseverance, of holding things up, of enduring. The silo board, once part of a structure that protected grain, had become something much more: a shelter for memories, a foundation for the generations he had nurtured.

Dad's gift wasn't just a keepsake. It was a reminder that the strongest legacies aren't built to be seen, but to be held, rooted, enduring, and deeply human. And in that truth, I find my own strength, carrying forward the quiet courage of a father who knew that love, like a silo, is built to withstand the storms.

A society that values youth often sees aging as a decline, a loss of energy to be resisted. But if we see the autumn leaf not as a sad surrender, but as a generous gift to the soil, we can think of our later years as a time of depth, reflection, and quiet grace.

Aging becomes an invitation to become a source of nourishment for those who come after us, our stories, our wisdom, our love, rather than a loss of value. Just as a seed hides in the dark, trusting the return of spring, we can trust that the quiet seasons of our lives are preparing us for a renewed flourishing, even if that flourishing will be seen in the lives of others.

Living the Call Daily

The call to care, therefore, is not a lofty, abstract ideal reserved for theologians or activists; it is a daily practice of being present, reverent, and intentionally caring. It is found in the moment we pause to thank God for the taste of fresh water, in the decision to plant a tree that will outlive us, in the simple act of holding a child's hand and naming the birds that sing overhead. It is in the breath we take before we speak, the silence we allow between words, the pauses that give space for the Holy Spirit to move.

When we approach each task, whether we are weeding a garden, feeding the stray cats on our porch, or mentoring a younger colleague, with the mindset that we are caring for a part of the divine tapestry, the ordinary becomes sacred. The biblical principle of "faithfulness in little things" transforms from an ethical guideline into a lived reality, a way of being that shapes our character and, in turn, influences the world around us.

The Heartbeat of the Master Plan

God's Master Plan isn't just about big declarations or amazing miracles; it's also in the little moments we often miss. It's in a grandparent's steady hand guiding a child's wobbly steps, in the shared laughter around a simple dinner, and in the peaceful quiet of a winter morning when the world seems to pause. It's there at the start of life, as we grow, age, and end, each stage a vital part of a divine song.

We're not meant to rush through life but to dance with it, moving smoothly from one moment to the next, trusting that every move, no matter how small, adds to the beautiful music of love that holds everything together. As we start to see the beauty in each leaf, each bee, each breath, we're drawn closer to the One who counts every hair on our heads. In that connection, we find our true home.

Closing Invitation

So, I stand here now, knowing I'm "next in line," not with fear, but with pride. I'm called to live each day as if it's a special season, full of light, meaning, and grace. I invite you to join me in this practice of being present: step outside, sit under a tree, listen to the whispers of the world, and let the small things teach you about the big love that makes everything work. By appreciating the little things, we become not just part of God's plan, but living examples of it, caretakers, witnesses, and cherished children of a Creator who loves every snowflake, every bee, and every heart that beats to His eternal song.

Photo Credit: Johannes Plenio on Unsplash

Sail boldly into the unknown, guided by steadfast faith and unshakable courage.

Chapter Twelve

Epilogue

Author of **Under the Midnight Sky**, THE FARM BOY WHO REACHED THE STARS: A TRUE STORY OF AMERICAN RESILIENCE, and I **Followed a Different Star**, THE FARM BOY WHO REACHED THE STARS; A TRUE STORY OF FAITH AND RESILIENCE.

A Journey Ignited by a Sandbox

I was born at the base of the gentle slopes that hug the highest point in Pennsylvania. The landscape was a patchwork of rolling fields, wind-tossed pine trees, and the low rumble of a dairy herd that never seemed to sleep. Our small farm perched there like a weather-worn barn on a hill, its red-painted doors creaking each time a gust of wind slipped through the open windows. I grew up with the scent of fresh milk, hay, and earth in my lungs, and with the rhythm of early-morning milking calls as my alarm clock.

I was the middle child of eight, six boys and two girls, each of us with a distinct role in the family's daily choreography. Somewhere between the roar of the milking machine and the soft hum of my mother's lullabies, I often found myself standing alone, a solitary figure in the middle of the chaos, with nothing but a head full of questions.

It was in these quiet interludes that my imagination took root. While the rest of the family tended to the chores, I would retreat to the small, battered sandbox that sat under the oak tree beside our house. The sand was my canvas, and my bare hands were the tools with which I built entire worlds. I traced winding roadways that cut through imagined mountains, raised concrete-like towers that scraped the sky, and drew sprawling towns where every house had a story. I gave each structure a name, "Cedar Point," "Silver Meadow," "Starfall," and populated them with invisible citizens who whispered their hopes, fears, and triumphs. I could feel the pulse of a bustling city, hear the clatter of market stalls, and sense the hum of a train that never left the sandbox. In those fleeting moments, I learned the most fundamental lesson of my life:

possibility begins in the mind, not the circumstance.

But stepping beyond the farm's boundary felt like entering a different world. By the time I hit seventh grade at our small public school, my name, Geoffrey, a straightforward name that seemed to suit a farmer just fine, was often mispronounced by Mrs. Whitaker (not her real name), the English teacher whose voice could dampen even the most eager student's enthusiasm. She'd call me "Goffrey," turning a simple hello into a subtle accusation that my identity didn't quite fit in her classroom. These mispronunciations weren't just a slip-up; they were a quiet, persistent reminder that I felt out of place, as if I didn't quite belong in the world of books, essays, and literary analysis.

I figured out that the only way to rewrite a story you're not in control of is to create your own story. I was not advised to take AP courses or to take the SAT as a college entry requirement. College seemed as far away as the stars I'd later watch from NASA's launch pads.

I started to see that learning isn't a straight line; it's a web of mentors, friends, mistakes, and little wins. My mom, who only went to eighth grade, tried to help me with my fourth-grade math.

When it was time to apply for college, my transcript wasn't great; it had a few farm-related things and three community college credits. I wrote essays that talked about the sandbox towns that taught me to handle complicated stuff, the milky mornings that made me disciplined, and the dreams of rockets that kept me looking ahead.

I got into a private university's engineering program, where I could finally combine my hands-on experience with theoretical study. The first semester was a culture shock. Professors used words that sounded like alien languages; labs needed precision I'd only practiced on a farm in a different way. But whenever I felt lost, I remembered the sandbox. I broke down each problem into "roads" and "structures," mapping out each step, and imagining electricity flowing like a river through a town I'd built in my mind. The same patience that made me wait hours for a cow to calm down now helped me align laser beams in a physics lab.

Five years after starting my college journey, I earned two degrees. I graduated quietly, realizing that my journey was shaped by the support of my family, friends, and mentors. The engineering degree eventually led me to a surprising opportunity at NASA's Johnson Space Center, where I helped establish a new Branch in the Avionics System Division. The move from a dairy farm to a space agency felt like stepping into another world. On my first day, I walked past the massive launch vehicles that launched the Apollo missions, the shiny white rockets that seemed like the ultimate playground, and I felt a strange calm wash over me. I was no longer just the kid who built sandcastles; I was now part of a team creating systems among the stars.

But that was just the beginning. Years of hard work, sleepless nights, and a burning curiosity pushed me forward. We moved from Johnson Space Center in Houston, Texas, to the political landscape of NASA Headquarters in Washington, D.C. I led teams that planned our future on the Moon, mentored interns from backgrounds similar to mine, and eventually became the Acting Associate Administrator of NASA's Science Mission Directorate.

What have I learned?

Imagination is the key to progress. The sandbox towns taught me to think about systems, foresee potential issues, and encourage creativity. When you let your mind explore beyond the obvious, you're planting the seeds for new ideas.

Mentors are more important than grades. Mrs. Whitaker's mistakes tried to silence me, but many others helped me find my voice. Find people who see the potential in you that you might not see in yourself yet.

Hard work is not limited by circumstances. The discipline of milking cows at dawn is the same determination needed to lead teams building observatories that are now traveling one million miles from Earth. Your background is not a limitation; it's a resource.

Childhood to rockets to NASA: What a journey

Now that I look back, I see that the farm, the sandbox, the funny name, and the teacher who didn't believe in me weren't obstacles; they were the things that built my strength. The hills of Mount Davis are still there, a reminder that the highest point in Pennsylvania isn't just a place; it's a symbol for every peak we try to reach.

If you're feeling lost on a dusty road, feeling invisible, and hearing voices telling you you'll never be more than a farmer, remember that the world is huge, and the stars are waiting for your name.

Bring your imagination with you, find mentors like a team of co-pilots, and aim for the sky. The journey from a small dairy farm to a senior executive at NASA might seem like a story from a book, but it's really about believing in yourself and never giving up—a story that anyone can tell, one small step at a time.

Retirement – a new story

For many, retirement means relaxing in the sun. But for some, it's a fresh start, a chance to explore and make a difference. Retirement isn't about being bored; it's about using what you know and love to do something new and exciting. That's how it has been for me since I finished my time at NASA.

After leaving NASA in 2016, I quickly joined the Johns Hopkins Applied Physics Lab, where I applied my skills to help with independent projects and proposals. But what really mattered was my desire to give back.

I've always believed that when you've been in a high-level government job, it's important to share what you've learned. My love for STEM+AD (Science, Technology, Engineering, Math plus Arts and Design) education led me straight into classrooms. I loved sharing my NASA story with middle and high school students, hoping to spark something in their minds.

One experience really stuck with me. A young girl in one of my classes doubted herself, saying she couldn't do much, and it hit me hard, reminding me of my own struggles in high school. That moment made me even more determined to help young people find their confidence and feel empowered.

Then, the COVID pandemic hit, and I found myself stepping into a new role: teaching a semester of Aerospace Engineering to junior and senior high school students. Naturally, most classes were online, but we did manage to chat about important topics in person when we could. I also brought in some fantastic guest speakers through online platforms: a Project Manager and Program Scientist who shared valuable skills and real-time examples from their work; an astronaut who shared his amazing experiences in space; even a Nobel Laureate who discussed his initial failures and eventual success through sheer tenacity and perseverance, and a cybersecurity expert who spoke about her educational challenges and the importance of cybersecurity today. I was determined to make the most of the online learning experience, and I was incredibly grateful for the heartwarming feedback

I received from the students at the end of the semester.

I challenged them with a paper exercise design project: build a Lunar hopper. The goal was to focus on objectives and design requirements, including environmental constraints, and design the hopper. I left plenty of room for creativity, but secretly included one unattainable requirement that over-constrained the design, without the students knowing the implications. They only discovered this challenge during our final in-person lesson! When they realized their design couldn't meet the requirements, we discussed real-life issues of unmet performance expectations and the need to reevaluate constraints. This "fail without failing" exercise was actually inspired by a previous discussion I had with astronaut Kathy Sullivan, who emphasized the importance of teaching students about persistence despite setbacks. At the end of the semester, students told me it was the most memorable lesson of all.

That whole experience really deepened my respect for educators. I witnessed firsthand that teaching demands significantly more time than is typically allotted for a single class. It is truly a labor of love!

Beyond the classroom, I joined the local school district's Citizen Financial Advisory Group, where I contributed my financial management expertise. And I answered the call to serve my community as a Town Commissioner, applying my knowledge to benefit local residents.

In 2019, NASA again sought my leadership, and I was honored to lead the independent review team for the Volatiles Investigating Polar Exploration Rover (VIPER) mission to the Moon. VIPER was designed to explore ice and other volatiles on the lunar surface and beneath it, gathering vital data for future lunar missions under the Artemis program. Sadly, the VIPER project was canceled due to funding challenges, affecting both the rover and the lander provided by the industry. At the same time, I co-led an independent review of NASA's Earth Observatory System plans, ensuring that Earth science satellites were well coordinated.

It's clear that retirement hasn't slowed me down! The shift to remote work during the pandemic allowed me to keep up with these various projects while still making time for family. Speaking of family, a trip to Las Vegas with my wife, Lauretta, was unforgettable. We saw an incredible Blue Man Group performance packed with surprises. A friend in Vegas arranged the tickets, but there was a special surprise in store.

We were told to arrive early for the show and were seated halfway back in the auditorium, with an aisleway directly behind us. We were a bit puzzled, wondering why our friend's "connections" hadn't gotten us better seats. But then, just before the show started, an usher came and asked us to follow him. As we walked across the aisle, a spotlight shone on us, and the music played, "You're late, you're late, you're holding up the show, you're late." It was a bit embarrassing, to say the least! We were then led to center seats, eight rows from the front. Later, we discovered that those closer than eight rows would get splattered with water during the show. After the performance, an usher kindly gifted us a pair of drumsticks used during the show. One of the Blue Man Group members even autographed the sticks for us, leaving his signature blue lip prints on them! It was such an exciting adventure!

After the Blue Man Group concert

Since then, Lauretta and I have had so many adventures, discovering new places and reliving happy family memories. We've visited Paris, taken cruises through the Alaskan inner passage, explored the Hawaiian Islands, and even sailed through the Panama Canal.

Now, I'm making a conscious effort to spend more time doing things I enjoy, mentoring students, spending quality time with my family, and starting to write about my experiences so I can really enjoy what I've achieved. But my love for space exploration and NASA's work is still strong. I even hosted Delaware Congressman Brian Pettyjohn at the Wallops Flight Facility for an Antares launch event, where we showed off the important work they do there.

In the middle of everything, I really want to spend more time with my family. I try to do this even though I'm mentoring students and getting involved in school activities. But it's often in special moments, like watching our grandson play hockey, that I really feel this desire. His love for the game is contagious, and seeing him with his cool, new composite stick and those amazing slap shots makes me think of my own teenage years on the ice. Those were simpler times, all about pure enthusiasm and the cold, where the "arena" was just a snow-covered patch of ice. Back then, we played with heavy wooden hockey sticks, and there was no talk of "flex points" or "kick points." You felt every bit of the puck on the blade, and you got power from your upper body and technique. Compared to our grandson's lightweight, high-performance stick, designed for super-fast whip and shots, it feels like a whole different world.

 As you start mapping out your own path, something wonderful happens: the story you share becomes a guiding light for others. Someone far away might read your words and feel that familiar pull, a gentle reminder that they, too, are not alone in their doubts, fears, or achievements. Your story becomes their window, and the story continues.

Picture a world where each of us, after reading a little bit of someone else's life, feels inspired to add our own verse to the grand poem of humanity. The chorus would be fuller, the harmonies more beautiful, and the pauses between verses less intimidating.

So, thank you for stepping into my world, for taking a moment to see a part of my journey. May that part have sparked a small flame, encouraging you to write your own. May the challenge feel less like a mountain and more like a steppingstone across a stream you've already walked in your mind.

Chapter Thirteen

Author

Two books highlighting the journey

I had the pleasure of writing two books that are companions to TREE TIME, which focus on my journey as a humble farm boy working in the dust of the family farm to the stars of NASA's Science Mission Directorate. My journey is a testament to the power of curiosity, grit, and one relentless question: *What if?* These pages, complemented by my two companion books, trace the unexpected path of a boy who was told he'd spend his life tending crops, but who instead found himself overseeing missions that explore the cosmos. It's a story not just of rockets and discoveries, but of roots, resilience, and the unshakable belief that even the humblest beginnings can launch boundless possibilities.

"With more than 16 years in the industry and 16 years at NASA, Geoff's story is not only of individual success and hard work, but also of NASA's transition to a new era of space exploration, in which he played many key leadership roles. He has accomplished what most of us come here hoping to do—move our mission—and America's space program—forward." *Former NASA Administrator, Retired Major General Charles F. Bolden Jr.*

"This poignant and comprehensive portrait of a life lived with passion, purpose, and profound belief reminds us that the greatest journeys are often those that transcend earthly boundaries, touching the very fabric of existence and revealing the boundless possibilities when one dares to follow a different star." Kaya Jones, artist, singer/songwriter, and Grammy Award winner

From dirt roads to deep space—one man's journey to the stars against all odds.

In this stirring memoir, Geoff Yoder shares his remarkable transformation from a struggling farm boy in western Pennsylvania to leading NASA's largest civilian space science organization.

This remarkable ascent, an improbable journey from the fields of his youth to the gleaming, high-tech corridors of NASA, masterfully illustrates how a young man, told he wouldn't amount to anything beyond his inherited plot of land, dared to look up and dream beyond the immediate horizon. Fueled by an unquenchable curiosity, the unwavering support of family and coworkers, and a relentless, almost fierce dedication to unraveling the cosmos's secrets, Geoff's path was one of audacious ambition against formidable odds.

Through raw reflection and hard-won wisdom, this book offers a powerful message: success isn't reserved for the chosen—it belongs to those who refuse to give up.

Perfect for dreamers, doers, and anyone ready to believe in their own impossible.

My published books

The Journey, Twice Told

Both books share the same Northstar—my passage from a doubtful child to a NASA senior executive—but they speak in different dialects.

Under The Midnight Sky is the sprint: fast, focused, perfect for the busy reader who wants to feel the rush of victory in a single breath.

I Followed a Different Star is the marathon: reflective, layered, a space where faith and physics dance together in the same orbit.

Read one, read both, and let the twin constellations guide you. Whether you need a quick lift or a lingering gaze, these stories are a beacon of hope for anyone who's ever been told they're not good enough—and a reminder that the brightest stars are often the ones that choose a different path.

www.ingramcontent.com/pod-product-compliance
Lightning Source LLC
Chambersburg PA
CBHW051832150726
47998CB00001B/384